1,000,000 Books
are available to read at

www.ForgottenBooks.com

Read online
Download PDF
Purchase in print

ISBN 978-1-334-27857-0
PIBN 10761225

This book is a reproduction of an important historical work. Forgotten Books uses state-of-the-art technology to digitally reconstruct the work, preserving the original format whilst repairing imperfections present in the aged copy. In rare cases, an imperfection in the original, such as a blemish or missing page, may be replicated in our edition. We do, however, repair the vast majority of imperfections successfully; any imperfections that remain are intentionally left to preserve the state of such historical works.

Forgotten Books is a registered trademark of FB &c Ltd.
Copyright © 2018 FB &c Ltd.
FB &c Ltd, Dalton House, 60 Windsor Avenue, London, SW19 2RR.
Company number 08720141. Registered in England and Wales.

For support please visit www.forgottenbooks.com

1 MONTH OF FREE READING

at

www.ForgottenBooks.com

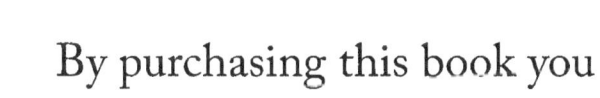

By purchasing this book you are eligible for one month membership to ForgottenBooks.com, giving you unlimited access to our entire collection of over 1,000,000 titles via our web site and mobile apps.

To claim your free month visit: www.forgottenbooks.com/free761225

* Offer is valid for 45 days from date of purchase. Terms and conditions apply.

English
Français
Deutsche
Italiano
Español
Português

www.forgottenbooks.com

Mythology Photography **Fiction** Fishing Christianity **Art** Cooking Essays Buddhism Freemasonry Medicine **Biology** Music **Ancient Egypt** Evolution Carpentry Physics Dance Geology **Mathematics** Fitness Shakespeare **Folklore** Yoga Marketing **Confidence** Immortality Biographies Poetry **Psychology** Witchcraft Electronics Chemistry History **Law** Accounting **Philosophy** Anthropology Alchemy Drama Quantum Mechanics Atheism Sexual Health **Ancient History** **Entrepreneurship** Languages Sport Paleontology Needlework Islam **Metaphysics** Investment Archaeology Parenting Statistics Criminology **Motivational**

Memoir.

NICHOLAS HILL was born in Florida, Montgomery County, in the year 1805. His grandfather, a native of Derry, Ireland, came to this country during the Colonial period, and settled in Schenectady. On the breaking out of the Revolution, his two sons, NICHOLAS and Henry, the former fourteen, the latter twelve years of age, ran away from home and joined the American army, with which they remained till the close of the war. It was the fortune of NICHOLAS to serve under the Commander-in-Chief, Washington, with whom he was at the final victory of Yorktown, and from whom he received a testimonial under his own signature, (now in the possession of the family) of his faithful services.

After the war, he settled in Florida, Montgomery County, where he remained till his death in 1856. In the middle period of his life, deeply impressed with religious sentiments, he became a preacher. He was a man of great physical strength, of great force of character, stern in

Memoir of

principle, pure in purpose, simple, yet impressively eloquent and earnest.

His son, NICHOLAS, inherited these traits; and his independent spirit and individuality of character led him to abandon home at an early age, and seek his fortune. He maintained himself by teaching school, surveying farms, &c., while he studied law, first in Montgomery County, afterwards in Schoharie, till, in August, 1829, he was finally admitted to the profession, and entered into partnership with DEODATUS WRIGHT, in Amsterdam. Shortly afterwards, Judge COWEN, of Saratoga, who was engaged in the preparation of notes to Phillips' Evidence, associated Mr. HILL with him. The work, which was the fruit of their joint labors, is one of great erudition, and of proportionate value to the profession. To Mr. HILL, the association with Judge COWEN was of important influence in the formation of his character, offering that example of singleness of purpose, devotion to his profession, and unwearied industry, upon which he modeled his own career. He became associated with SIDNEY J. COWEN, a son of the Judge, with THOMAS J. MARVIN, with WILLIAM A. BEACH, and with Mr. BELDING, his brother-in-law. On removing to Albany, he again became associated with DEODATUS WRIGHT, and with Mr. NASH; but in the latter part of 1840 he was appointed State Reporter, which place he held till 1845, publishing, during this term, a series of volumes

Nicholas Hill.

which constitute some of the most valuable of the New York Reports.

On the termination of his office, he entered into partnership with PETER CAGGER, and the firm, with which JOHN K. PORTER was soon afterwards associated, continued till his death. He so systematised his business as to be able to devote all his time and thoughts to the higher pursuits of the law. He gave to it all his faculties and all his heart, and, loving it for its own sake, and not for its rewards, achieved in it a position commensurate with his devotion. Though at one time nominated for representative in Congress, and at another for Judge of the Court of Appeals, he was never an aspirant for office, and was only interested in politics as they involved the great constitutional questions with which his studies made him familiar, and to the understanding of which his mind had been trained, or as they enlisted that strong sentiment of patriotism which he inherited from his revolutionary father, and which nothing ever effaced.

The fame achieved in professional life leaves behind it but few records; and even the notes of decisions and the volumes of reports furnish very inadequate means of judging of the comparative standing or success of lawyers. It is not too much to say that, by the common consent of the bar, Mr. HILL stood foremost among the first. He was associated in all the leading cases that arose in his time,

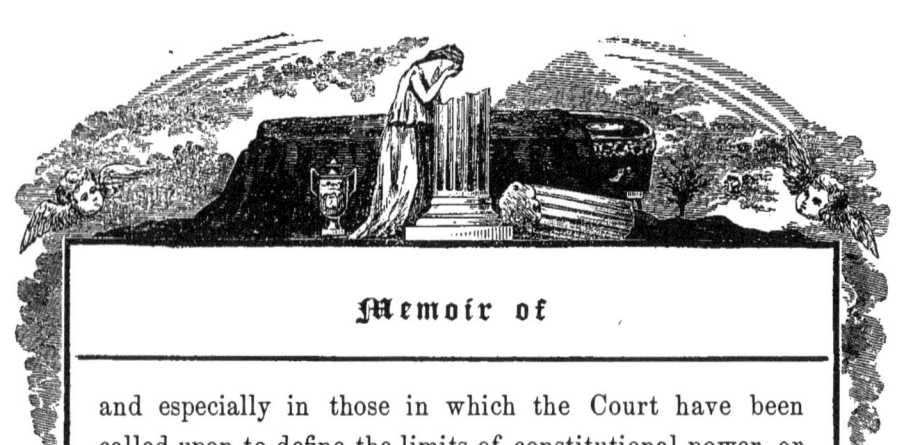

Memoir of

and especially in those in which the Court have been called upon to define the limits of constitutional power, or defend the rights of citizens and communities.

Of late years, the habit of profound legal research grew upon him; and with the feelings of a true lawyer, he gave himself up to the study of each case before him, without reference to the amount or magnitude of personal interests at stake, so much as to the delicacy of the questions presented, and the character of the legal principles involved. When devoting himself to such questions, the labors of a long day were often prolonged far beyond midnight, to recommence anew in the morning, and be thus continued for months. And yet, with all this devotion to his profession, he was not indifferent to social life, nor incapable of appreciating and contributing to its pleasures. He preserved his youthfulness of feeling, his freshness of heart, his noble simplicity of character to the last. The perfect purity of his life, and his singleness of ambition, in which he was so successful, placed him above all temptations. He could not be petty or unfair, or disingenuous. He could not espouse a bad cause, nor take an unfair advantage of an opponent, nor mislead the Court. He did not court wealth or power. He loved good men, and natures frank like his own. He loved good books, and often turned aside from his studies to commune with the great thinkers by whom the

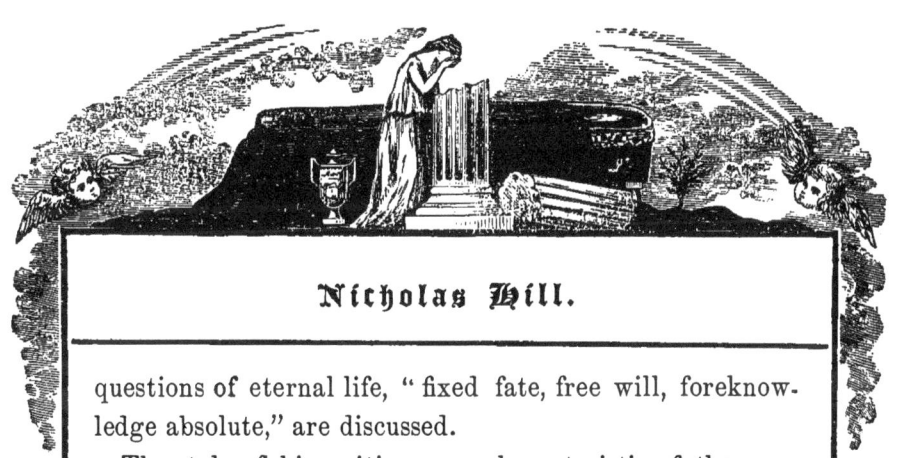

Nicholas Hill.

questions of eternal life, " fixed fate, free will, foreknowledge absolute," are discussed.

The style of his writing was characteristic of the man. His points of argument indicated great powers of analysis and remarkable labor ; but his argument was simple, lucid, forcible, enriched by illustrations from history and literature, and imbued with the spirit of legal philosophy.

In spite of his devoted labors, his life was a happy one. He loved his profession, and was successful in it. He drew around him the ablest men in its ranks, and enjoyed their affection and confidence.

Though occasionally his mind gave signs of weariness, it never failed, after a brief interval of leisure, to resume its accustomed elasticity ; and it was only when it gave way altogether that his friends became conscious of the overwrought tension to which it had been subjected. He died on Sunday morning, May 1st, 1859, in the fifty-fourth year of his age, after an illness of a few days, the first threatening symptoms of which appeared to give way, affording hope of recovery, until that last moment in which his spirit, serene and clear in its faculties, suddenly took flight.

He was buried on the third day of May, 1859, the Judges of the Court of Appeals and the members of the bar from Albany, and from other cities of the State, attending his remains to the grave.

He was not old when he died, yet he was so superior

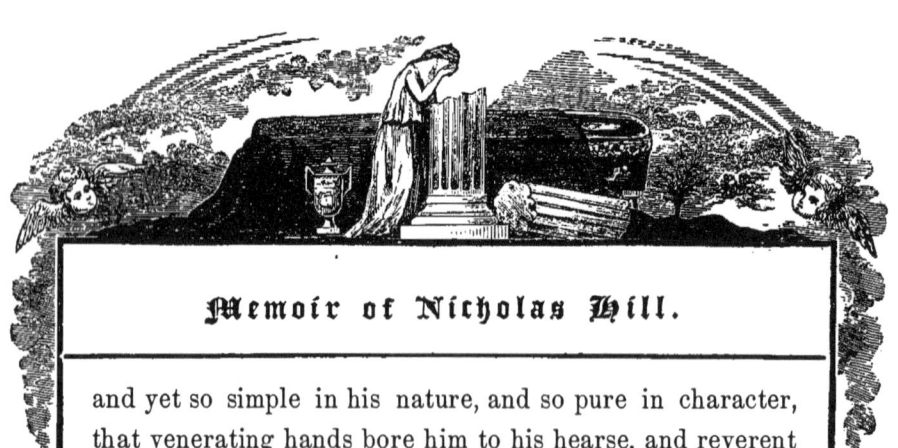

Memoir of Nicholas Hill.

and yet so simple in his nature, and so pure in character, that venerating hands bore him to his hearse, and reverent footsteps followed him to his tomb, as if the sanctities of age had hallowed his life before its close ; and yet warm hearts will cherish his memory with all the ardors of youthful love and remembrance.

Proceedings of the New York Bar.

AT a meeting of the bar of the city of New York, held at the Hall of the Supreme Court, on the 26th day of May, 1859, convened in consequence of the death of NICHOLAS HILL, Esq., at Albany,

On motion of Mr. JOHN MCKEON,

Mr. Justice NELSON, of the Supreme Court of the United States, was called to the chair.

On motion of Mr. JOHN VAN BUREN,

Judge BETTS, United States District Court; Mr. Justice ROOSEVELT, Presiding Justice Supreme Court; Chief Justice BOSWORTH, Superior Court; and First Judge DALY, Common Pleas, were appointed Vice-Presidents.

On motion,

Mr. CHARLES TRACY and Mr. DANIEL D. LORD were appointed Secretaries.

MR. JUSTICE NELSON,

on taking the chair, addressed the meeting as follows:

GENTLEMEN OF THE BAR: We have met to pay our respects to the memory of our deceased brother, NICHOLAS

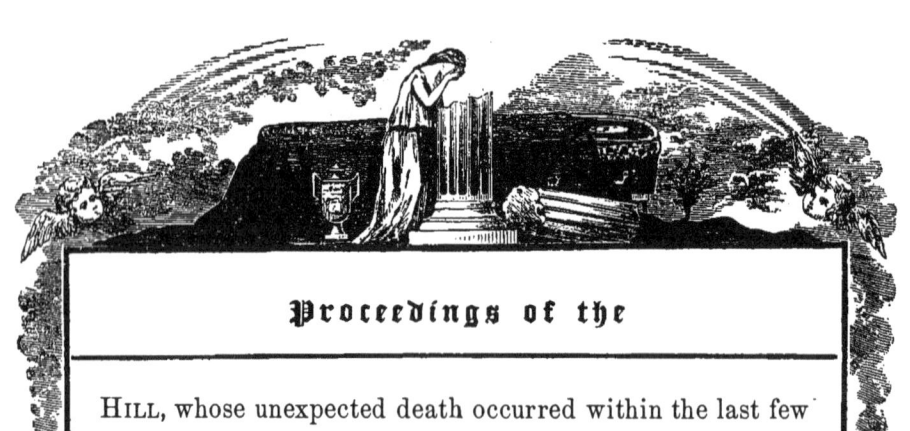

Proceedings of the

HILL, whose unexpected death occurred within the last few days. I have known Mr. HILL ever since he came into the profession, and have witnessed his advance to distinction until he had reached and stood in the very front rank of the bar of New York. He was a man of a bright mind, and of most indefatigable industry—an industry and devotion to his profession which may well be regarded as an example to the junior members of the bar. And eminent and distinguished as he was in his profession, he was, if possible, still more so in the walks of private life, for high social qualities, especially when mingling with his professioual brethren, and, under all circumstances and in all places, for the sternest integrity and honor. We deplore his loss, and take a melancholy pleasure in presiding over a meeting of his professional brethren, assembled to do honor to his memory.

Mr. J. W. EDMONDS offered the following

Resolutions:

Resolved, That in the death of NICHOLAS HILL, an eminent member of our profession, distinguished as the leading counsel in our court of dernier resort, the profession throughout the whole State have to deplore the loss of a brother, endeared to most of them by professional as well as personal relations, and whose exalted merits as a lawyer were known to and estimated by all.

New York Bar.

Resolved, That in the recollection of his untiring industry, his uniform courtesy of deportment, his sterling integrity, and the acuteness and expansion of his legal mind, he has left us a memorial of professional attributes worthy alike of our admiration and our imitation.

Resolved, That we deeply sympathize with the Judges of the Court of Appeals, and with our brethren of the bar at the capitol, in the loss which they and we have alike sustained, and that we will unite with others in asking at the hands of that Court a proper testimonial of our common regard to his memory.

Resolved, That a committee be appointed, on behalf of the bar of New York, to communicate to that Court the sentiments here expressed.

MR. CHARLES O'CONOR,

in seconding the resolutions, addressed the meeting as follows:

MR. CHAIRMAN: In the death of NICHOLAS HILL, our profession and the circle of our private friendships have suffered a great loss. I would fain indulge in silence the emotion it excites; but this may not be. His eminent virtues demand a public tribute, and though incapable of doing full justice to them, I must contribute my mite to the present testimonial.

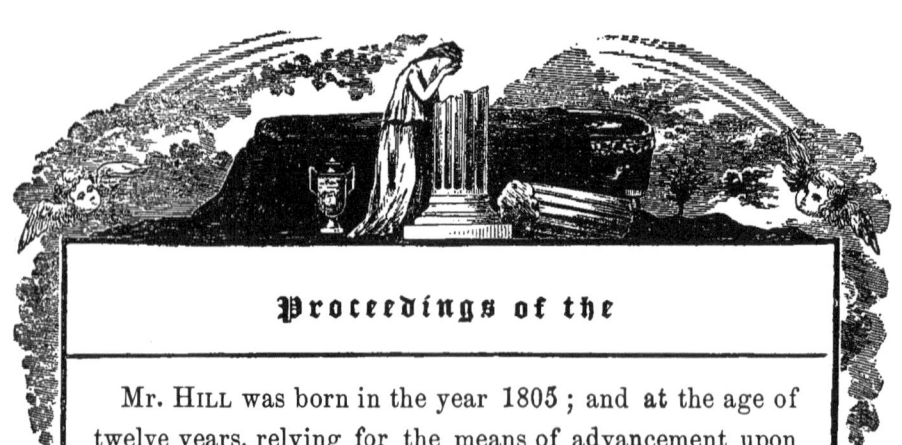

Proceedings of the

Mr. HILL was born in the year 1805; and at the age of twelve years, relying for the means of advancement upon his own unaided industry, he went forth from the home of his youth, intent upon a career of honorable usefulness. Our profession was his chosen pursuit; and even in the associations of his novitiate, he developed the same wisdom which marked his actions in after life. The library of DANIEL CADY, the foremost lawyer in northern New York, was the theatre of his earliest studies. That he was not less modest, patient and assiduous, than enterprising, is proven at every stage of his journey through life. He abstained from taking an admission to practice as an attorney until twelve years of diligent study had thoroughly stored his mind with the principles of judicial science. He took the first degree in 1829, and was admitted to the bar in 1833.

He commenced his professional practice in a remote country village; but he soon removed to Saratoga Springs, where, amidst a circle of learned and laborious jurists, with their example to cheer him onward, and their vast libraries to feed his increasing eagerness for the acquisition of knowledge, he laid the deep and solid foundations of that learning for which he became so distinguished.

Twenty-five years only of professional life were accorded to him; but in that space how much he accomplished. First, let us contemplate the long term necessarily occu-

New York Bar.

pied by the young lawyer in approving himself as worthy of confidence, by the severe test of actual experience, under the eyes of the bench, the bar, and the public; then the progression, steady and gradual, as it must always be if accomplished at all, from an estimation, merely local and partial, to extended fame—the indispensable basis of high professional success. In some instances these steps seem to be achieved rapidly, each as it were at a single bound; but in our profession an advance of this kind is generally unreal. In Mr. HILL's career each step was taken deliberately and on firm ground; each advance was marked with substantial fruits.

Whilst at Saratoga Springs, he performed a large part in that gigantic task, the Notes upon PHILLIPS' Evidence. Whole libraries were taken up, and their contents reproduced in a form the most useful to the bench and the practitioner that could have been devised. Years of incessant toil were requisite to the completion of this work.

We next find him as State Reporter, immersed in the irksome task of bringing forth order from chaotic masses of that hardly legible manuscript in which our law papers were usually prepared at that time. Seven volumes of reports, prepared with unsurpassed judgment and fidelity, attest his skill, learning and diligence, during this period. They have incorporated his name with the judicial history of our State.

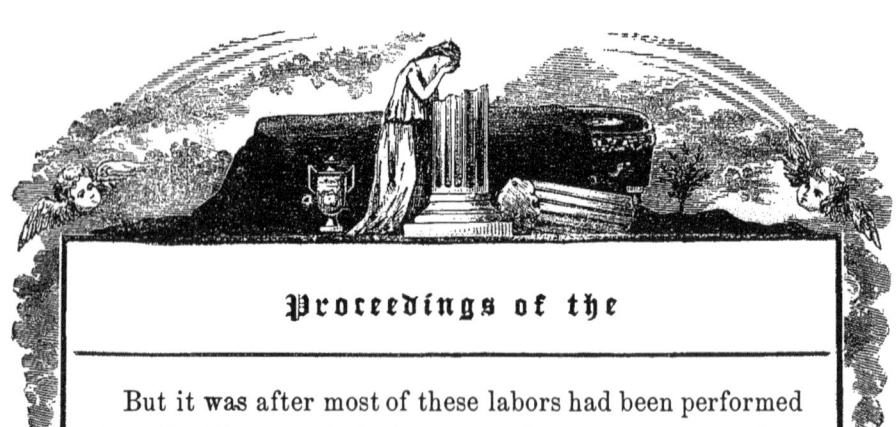

Proceedings of the

But it was after most of these labors had been performed that Mr. HILL reached the personal eminence as an advocate and a juris-consult, which brings home most distinctly to us the deep feeling of regret we this day experience. Retiring from the office of Reporter, Mr. HILL thenceforth devoted himself exclusively to practice at the bar.

This was his true position. The qualities here exhibited may not carry his renown to future times as effectually as his contributions to our legal literature, but they won for him the universal admiration of his cotemporaries, and the love of all who were so fortunate as to enjoy his society.

When summoned from earth, though he had only attained his fifty-third year, he held confessedly the first place at our bar.

A purity of life that knew no blemish, an integrity that no man ever impeached, even in thought, a love of justice that shone out in every word he uttered. as an advocate, or as an adviser, a calm, clear-sighted investigating intellect — ripened to fullest maturity and energy by fixed habits of intense application—which never left, in any case, a relevant fact undiscovered, or overlooked a pertinent legal principle : these, Mr. Chairman, were some of the qualities which secured NICHOLAS HILL the applause of all, and the unhesitating confidence of our highest judicial tribunal.

Commanding universal respect, the field of political eminence was ever open to him ; but with characteristic

New York Bar.

modesty he shunned its invitations. To the urgency of parties for his acceptance of nominations to office, he constantly returned denials. His official experience was indeed remarkable. Over-persuaded to take the office of District Attorney, whilst residing in Saratoga County, he soon relinquished it. Assuming, at the earnest solicitation of the Court, the honorable though painfully laborious office of State Reporter, he resigned it at the first moment a capable successor would be found. When it was thought fit to revise the existing practice of our courts, Mr. HILL was chosen by the Legislature as one of the Commissioners. For once he assumed office with readiness. His active benevolence saw an opportunity to do the people service, and he sat down to the task with the alacrity which always marked his entrance upon any field of useful labor. He spread out before his capacious mental ken the whole existing practice. He determined "to subject it to a free and thorough, though discriminating process of revision and amendment, retaining such parts of it as experience had proved to be really useful, and rejecting or reforming the rest." I use his own words. Different views, however, prevailed, and Mr. HILL resigned. "I am unwilling," said he, "to remain longer in a position where it is impossible for me to render any valuable service to the State." Those who concur in his views of expediency will see in this another proof of his far-seeing sagacity. All must concede

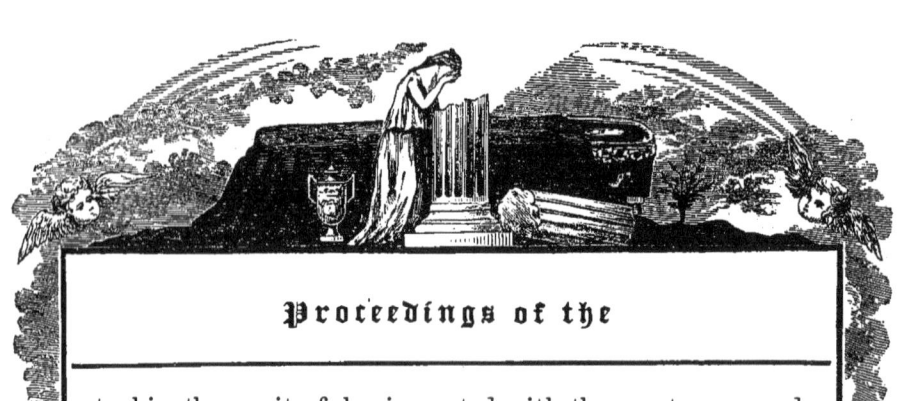

Proceedings of the

to him the merit of having acted with the most pure and patriotic motives.

He never subsequently accepted any public station; and the ten succeeding years formed the most brilliant portion of his life. Constantly occupied in the court of ultimate resort, and holding a brief on one side of every important cause before that high tribunal, he was brought into intimate professional and social relations with the whole bar of our State. And here it was that his merits shone out with their highest lustre. To the admiration which had been won by extensive learning, profound judgment and unwearied industry, was now added love for his kind and amiable character. How he gained upon all hearts, I have not language to describe. In the signs of emotion exhibited around me, I feel that the memory of my hearers recalls the proof, and amply supplies my deficiencies.

Still I must relate a single incident. When in the full tide of his professional success, during one of the Spring terms of the Supreme Court, held in this city, Mr. HILL was placed upon the committee to examine applicants for admission. Among the candidates were two young gentlemen who, in the stern judgment of Mr. HILL's associates, failed to exhibit the requisite acquirements. The decision was undeniably just; even NICHOLAS HILL could not argue against its justice; but he felt, and he said that it was cruel. The young men were strangers to him, but they

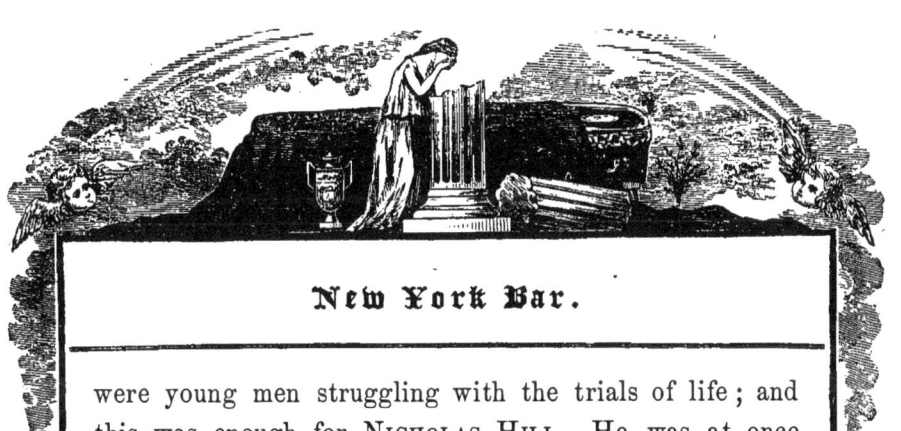

New York Bar.

were young men struggling with the trials of life; and this was enough for NICHOLAS HILL. He was at once transformed from the austere champion of justice, as he was known at the bar, to the suppliant for a gentler result. To his manly intellect there seemed to be conjoined a woman's heart. He besought his associates to a kindlier conclusion, as a mother would crave indulgence to the failings of a beloved son.

In the last dread trial to which he has passed, perhaps that effort of his benignant and merciful temper may have carried with it a far richer blessing than the lofty intellect which secured him so many earthly triumphs.

It greatly deepens our regret at his decease that Mr. HILL'S capacity for professional labor seemed to have been in no degree impaired. Many years of usefulness appeared to be in store for him. During the last term of the Court of Appeals he argued a greater number of cases than at any previous sitting of the Court. On Saturday, the 23d of April, he visited his office for the last time. At eight o'clock in the morning, he commenced his preparation for the argument of a cause at the ensuing term of the Court of Appeals. Eleven hours of continuous application manifested the unimpaired vigor of his mind and body. Upon the following day, an indisposition occurred, which at first created no alarm, and for a time improvement was hoped for. But he was unable to leave his house during the

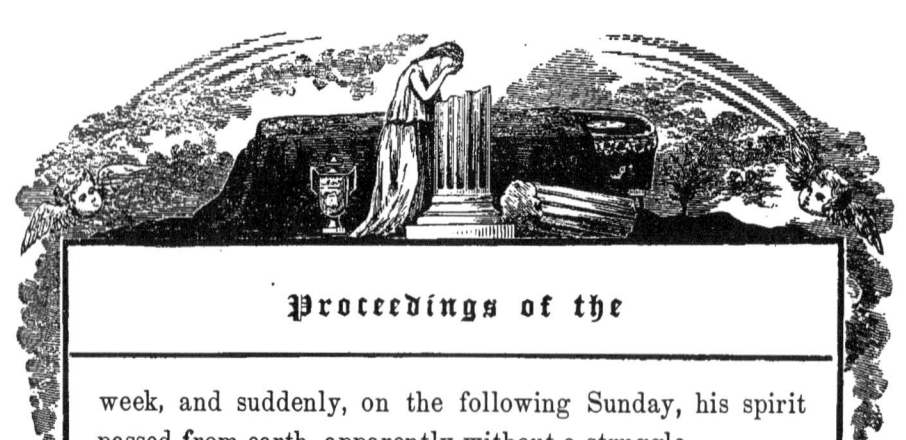

Proceedings of the

week, and suddenly, on the following Sunday, his spirit passed from earth, apparently without a struggle.

Such, seniors of the bar, was the brother whose loss we deplore. Such, juniors of the profession, was the bright model of which you have been deprived. Such, gentlemen students, was the friend of your class, whose kind spirit is no longer left to encourage your progress, to smooth your path onward, or, in the hour of trial, to cast in your favor the weight of his influence.

The motion was further supported by

MR. JAMES W. GERARD,

who spoke as follows:

This is the first time that I have ever taken part in any meeting of the bar, convened to pronounce eulogium upon the memory of one of its deceased members, although they have lately fallen around me like the autumnal leaves of the dying year. I have always sat a silent listener to the addresses of others, and have been content in the quiet corner of the court room to reflect within myself upon the passing scene, and upon the merits and memory of the departed brother.

It requires a nicely balanced mind, and a well regulated sympathy in a speaker, upon such an occasion. *Too much* feeling will render the eulogist unequal to the task; and

New York Bar.

his overcharged heart will not allow him to do justice to the subject, while the words of him who has *too little* feeling, will fall coldly and listlessly upon the ear. The just medium must be carefully observed by which the speaker shall refrain from fulsome compliment on the one hand, and cold praise on the other.

It is therefore with a perfect consciousness of the delicacy of the task that I have yielded to the solicitation of the gentlemen who have convened this meeting, to cast my stone upon the *cairn* which this meeting shall erect to the memory of one whom none knew but to honor, whom none spoke of but to praise.

The esteemed advocate who has preceded me has well portrayed the legal acquirements, the unwearied industry, the indefatigable energy of our deceased friend, by which he justly attained the front rank in the championship of the bar.

He has well described Mr. HILL as the profound lawyer, the clear commentator, the accurate Reporter. He has well painted that devoted fidelity to the interests of his clients by which he made every cause his own ; and whether it involved great or small pecuniary interest, was analyzed with an industry, and weighed so nicely in the scales of judicial authority, as to bring out in bold relief its elements of success. He has adverted with touching truthfulness to that honorable ambition by which this enthusiast

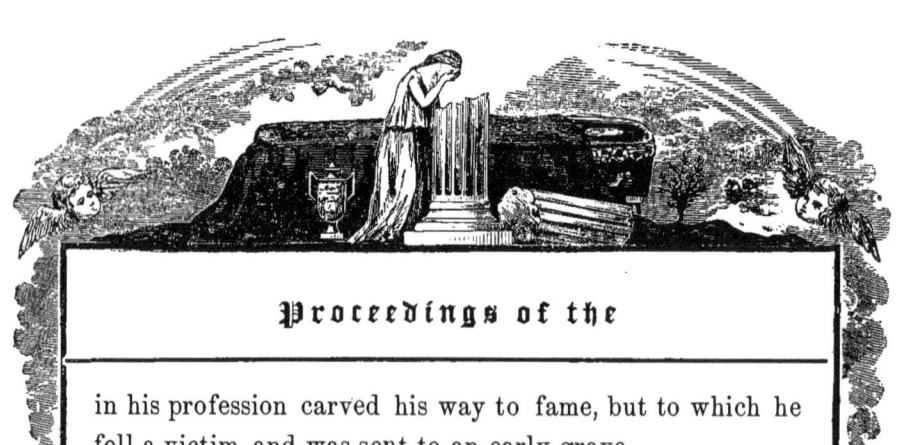

Proceedings of the

in his profession carved his way to fame, but to which he fell a victim, and was sent to an early grave.

It was my fortune, many years ago, to have encountered Mr. HILL as an opponent, in the first cause of magnitude with which he ever was intrusted; and the zeal, intelligence and legal knowledge which he evinced on that occasion first brought him into public notice, and laid the foundation of his future fame. It was an exciting contest between antagonistic parents for the custody of an infant child. It was a case which led to angry debate, and being one which involved the novel question of parental rights, largely engaged the public attention. The arena was the shaded grove of Chancellor Walworth's mansion, in the beautiful village of Saratoga Springs, and many strangers who had congregated at that fashionable watering-place, thronged the little court room, and eagerly listened to the novel and exciting debate. Mr. HILL, representing the father, had thoroughly stored his mind with all the book learning of the common law of England, and piled his authorities one upon the other mountain high, in favor of the father's paramount claim to the custody of his child. But the improved spirit of the age, the change in the tone of society in regard to the domestic relations of husband and wife, and parent and child, and the respect in the present day conceded to woman's intelligence, prevailed over the black letter law of past centuries, and the claims

New York Bar.

of the mother prevailed. (8 Paige R. 47, Barry *vs*. Mercein.) Throughout the whole of that exciting law-suit, which lasted for many years, on appeal through the several courts of the State, and in very many other cases in which Mr. HILL and myself were opposed, there had never passed between us one angry word, or a departure from that delicate courtesy and respect to his antagonist which so distinguished him in his professional career. Whether victory perched upon the banner of the one or the other, our friendship was never shaken by any exultation of triumph over him who was defeated.

The *last* cause in which I encountered him in the legal arena was one recently in the Court of Appeals, involving a large amount of property, and great questions of legal interest. He was brought into the cause rather hastily, and not long before the argument. Full points had been sent to him. An ordinary lawyer would have done his duty, and would have been satisfied to make the argument upon the platform laid out for him. Not so Mr. HILL. He threw them aside, and with infinite labor, in two days produced new points, most scientifically elaborated, on a case spread over a large volume. I had the last word in the argument, and summoned to my side all the power I was master of to beat down his views. When I had finished, he said to me, with a diffidence always allied to merit, that he felt that he had not done justice to his

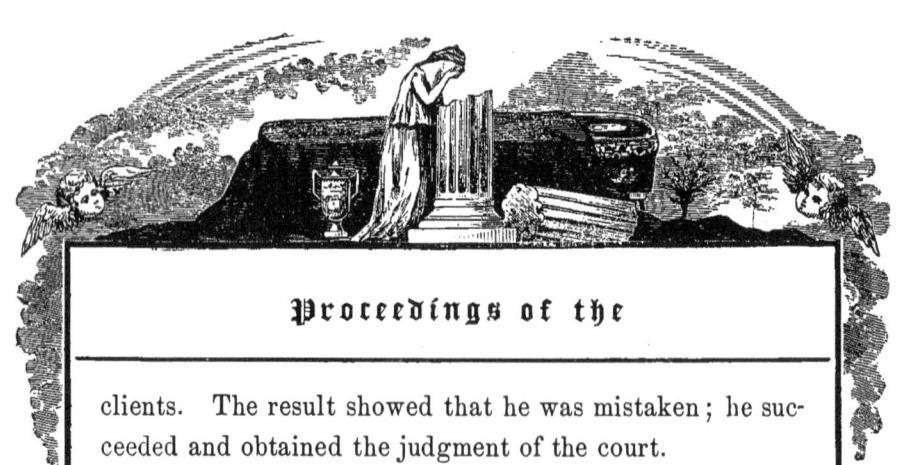

Proceedings of the

clients. The result showed that he was mistaken; he succeeded and obtained the judgment of the court.

But it is superfluous to speak of and to eulogize our friend's *legal* acquirements, the knowledge of which is co-extensive with the State, and is familiar to every member of our extensive bar. It is of Mr. HILL's character as a *man* and as a *friend* that I would speak—of the qualities of the *heart*, rather than the head—of his courteous demeanor as a high-toned gentleman—as one of nature's noblemen—of one who had a soul—who possessed human sympathy in an eminent degree, and whose heart overflowed with love and kindness for his friends. These were traits in his character beyond his profession which shone out conspicuously to those who knew him best, and which gave a lustre and a charm to his legal learning.

It was when he laid aside his legal harness, and in social converse among his intimates in private life, that the fine qualities of his character broke out, and a mind all intelligence and a soul all sympathy rose superior to the black letter lawyer of the courts. Then he threw from him for the while his *Coke* and his *Lyttleton*, his *Blackstone* and his *Bacon*, and as the social gentleman and warm friend, would discourse on topics of art or science, of taste and travel; and no man could be in his society and hear him philosophise on such subjects, without improvement, as well as pleasure.

New York Bar.

He would love to listen to accounts of *Europe*; its statuary, its paintings, its architecture and institutions, its history and political associations, and would lament that he had never had the time and opportunity of visiting these scenes of his imagination, and judge of them for himself. His ardent desire was that he might one day be able to revel amid those subjects which it was his delight to read of, and hear described by those who had been among them.

He had a passion for spending a large portion of almost every summer at the sea-side, and I have often passed pleasant days with him in social converse on the broad piazza of the Pavilion at Rockaway.

There he would gaze upon the restless sea, and watch the rolling billow as it came, and listen to its ceaseless roar; the *sea*, whose waves had rolled and rolled from creation's dawn, and would not cease to roll till chaos came again. There would his eye linger upon the setting sun, casting far upon the waste of water its golden hues, and lighting up with its tinted fires the crest of the rising billow. There would he watch wave chasing wave, from the gentle swell that, far out at sea, first formed itself, and growing as it approached, and raising its towering head, would dash itself upon the shore, and then be lost for ever. Such, he moralized, was human life; new-born generations chasing before them those who had just filled the high

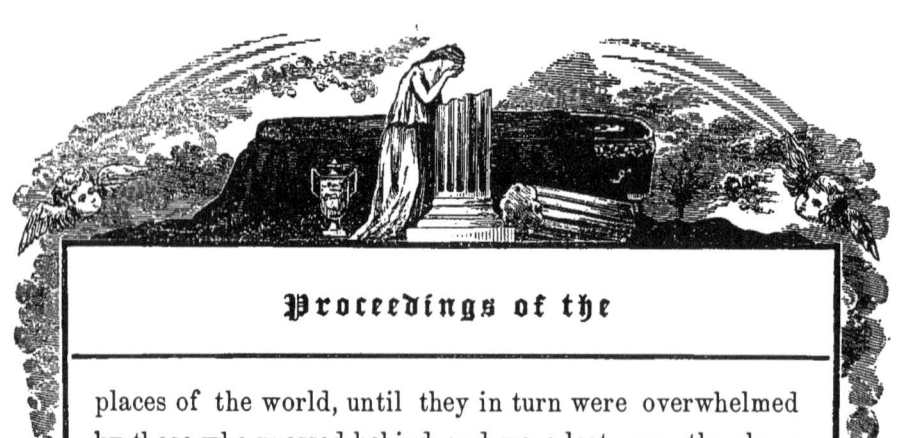

places of the world, until they in turn were overwhelmed by those who pressed behind, and were lost upon the shore of eternity. And then the departing sun (like the good man whose character lives after him) would send upwards far into the summer clouds its last setting beams, and gild the upper sky by its reflected glories, long after it had ceased to shine *directly* on the scene.

Let not the world suppose that the dusty volumes of the dry law choke the imagination, eradicate sentiment, or smother human sympathy. No man enjoys nature more than the educated lawyer out of court. Just in proportion as he is pressed down by the cares and anxieties of his profession, when the pressure is removed, his natural sympathies and feelings will rise with increased elasticity. In a word, we may say of our friend, *humanly* speaking, that his professional and private character were perfect; there was no blot upon his escutcheon.

To the younger members of the bar who hear me, I would hold up Mr. HILL as a marked example for their imitation. I would impress upon their minds this great truth—the possession of talents without private worth and good character only serve to render the possessor a more conspicuous mark for criticism and invective. That lawyer who addresses a court or jury, to convince or persuade, with a consciousness of a high individual character, feels in that consciousness a tower of strength; he is armed

with mail, not vulnerable; no, not even in the heel. And the young lawyer will soon learn that a Judge and jury will yield a deference to the opinions and arguments of such an advocate, which gives him a mighty advantage over the counsel upon whom and whose arguments the Judge and jury look with prejudice. The law is a noble profession to pursue; but the lawyer, by his power in that profession, may prove a curse or a blessing to his fellow-men; a sword to pierce, or a shield to protect. Mr. HILL's private character and private worth gave him great advantages and commanding influence over juries and Judges, whom he was in the habit of addressing.

To his immediate family, his sudden loss is irreparable: no language of sympathy can soothe the agonies of its bereaved members. All we can say is, "let the stricken deer go weep." A year since, I became acquainted with the only son of our friend, like him in form and feature, and I trust that he may be like him in character. I was most favorably impressed by him. May his father's mantle fall upon him; may it fit him, and may he wear it gracefully.

Mr. JAMES T. BRADY said:

MR. PRESIDENT: If I consulted my discretion alone, I would abstain from speaking on the present occasion, but this might seem to exhibit want of consideration for the

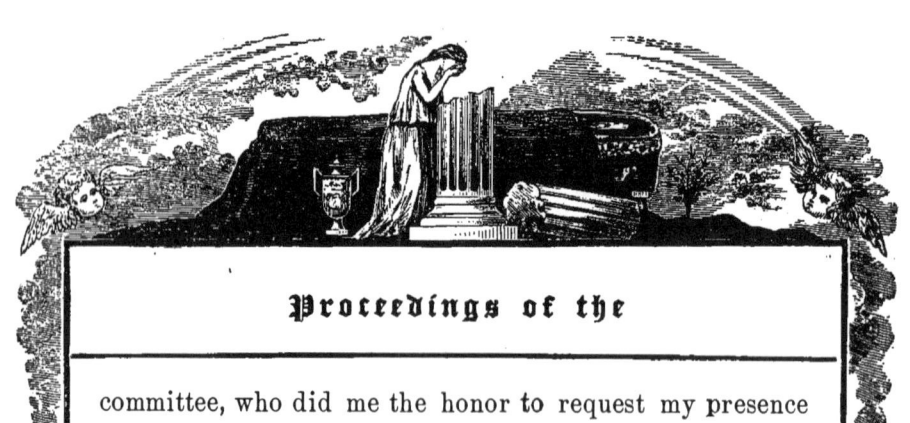

Proceedings of the

committee, who did me the honor to request my presence here, and I will utter a few words about our departed brother. What I have felt, now feel, and must feel hereafter, in contemplating the decease of Mr. HILL, it is not in my power adequately to express. I admired, respected, loved him. He deserved in an eminent degree whatever of either feeling might be entertained for him; and from our ranks, so often assailed of late by the fell destroyer, no victim could have been selected by Death whose sacrifice could awaken deeper or stronger sensations in our hearts.

Like many others present, I made the acquaintance of our brother at a period when the terms of the Courts of Errors and Chancery, and of the Supreme Court, brought together lawyers from every part of our State. We had then a State bar, ere changes, in this respect to be deplored, disturbed and perhaps terminated for ever the fraternal associations which existed under our former judicial system. We look back upon those by-gone days with mingled pleasure and regret. They were to me the halcyon hours of professional life, and from the retrospect which relumes them, many a recollection gleams forth of social and cheerful reunion. But as the light thus flashed from memory swiftly dies out, there appear in the succeeding gloom the names of the unforgotten departed, the companions of our "golden prime," the eloquent and successful GRAHAM; the terse and caustic DE WITT; the zealous

New York Bar.

and persevering BLUNT; the quiet and learned DODGE; but I will not complete the list of our brothers from the bar of this city, passed away from us for ever and for ever. With all these Mr. HILL was familiar; by all of them he was properly appreciated. All of us admired his fine intellect, thorough research, untiring industry, clear analysis, and mature judgment. All of us loved the genial, simple, affectionate and truthful qualities of his kindly nature. Who can ever forget his modesty? Who has not seen him when he rose entirely prepared to instruct and convince a court to illustrate his power, enrich jurisprudence, and adorn his own fame? Who has not seen him at such a moment with a blush upon his cheek, warm, truthful and natural, as that which tinges the features of the startled girl? With how much gratitude do many of us remember his generous conduct toward those with whom he was associated in an argument. He spared no pains to make his colleague acquainted with all that his own masterly preparation had secured. If that colleague faltered or stumbled, our brother cheered him on, and with strong intellectual grasp upheld him, pointing ever to the right path, and emitting over its every step, from the fullness of his own enlightenment, " the gladsome lights of jurisprudence." And now this great lawyer, warm-hearted friend, amiable companion, kind and faithful brother, and excellent man, is gone—gone far too early in life—gone while yet in the

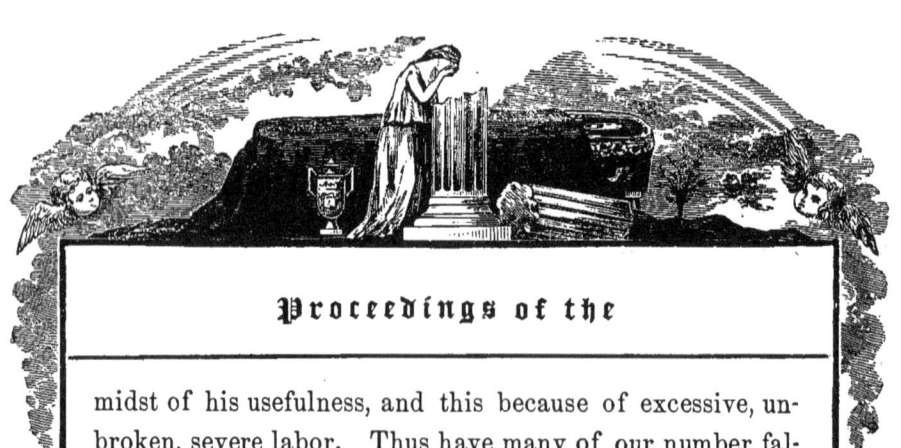

Proceedings of the

midst of his usefulness, and this because of excessive, unbroken, severe labor. Thus have many of our number fallen, and thus we have reason to apprehend that others may go from us, unless admonished by frequent instances, they let the over-tasked brain have occasional and refreshing repose, and feel that attention to health is entirely compatible with fully satisfying all the demands of duty.

To our cherished brother, HILL, let us breathe another farewell, and utter the fervent prayer that as he was deservedly honored and loved in this life, so may he be happy and glorious in the life to come.

Mr. STEPHEN P. NASH

then spoke as follows:

MR. CHAIRMAN: The fact that while I was a student at law, and for some years following, my relations with Mr. HILL were quite intimate, and that what I then learned of him may add something to the general estimate of his character, will, I trust, be considered an excuse for detaining this assembly a few moments longer.

I was still a school-boy when, about the year 1833, Mr. HILL came to Saratoga Springs, to enter on the preparation of that edition of "Phillips on Evidence," with which his name is now connected, and on which Judge COWEN had already made considerable progress. He must then

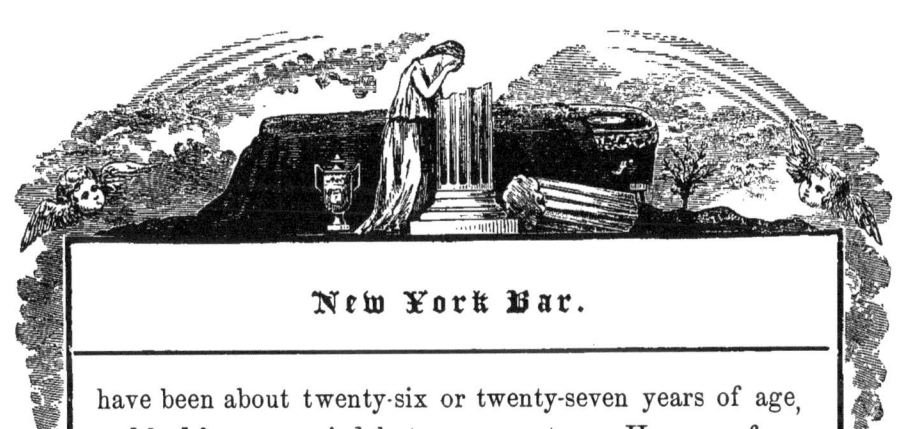

New York Bar.

have been about twenty-six or twenty-seven years of age, and had been married but a year or two. He came from Amsterdam, where he had practised law for a short time with the Hon. DEODATUS WRIGHT, now of Albany, and lately one of the Justices of the Supreme Court in the Third District.

The work on which Mr. HILL was engaged was already far advanced when I entered Judge COWEN's office as a student. I was soon called upon to aid in the correction of proof sheets, the verifying of citations, and other similar labor, and was thus brought into close observation of Mr. HILL's daily toil. In reference to this period of his life, it is perhaps sufficient to say that it was one of incessant, laborious and faithful industry.

The spot was favorable to such a life. Judge COWEN's offices and library were at the foot of his garden, in a retired part of the village. A stone building, between an outer office fronting on the street, and a rear room opening into the garden, held the library, Judge COWEN's pride, as the fear of its loss by fire was his great anxiety. In the outer office, Judge COWEN's son was engaged at such intervals as the practice of his profession allowed him, in the preparation of an enlarged edition of the Justice's "Court Manual," which his father in early life had published. The inner room was occupied by Judge COWEN and Mr. HILL. In this quiet spot, Mr. HILL laid broad and deep the founda-

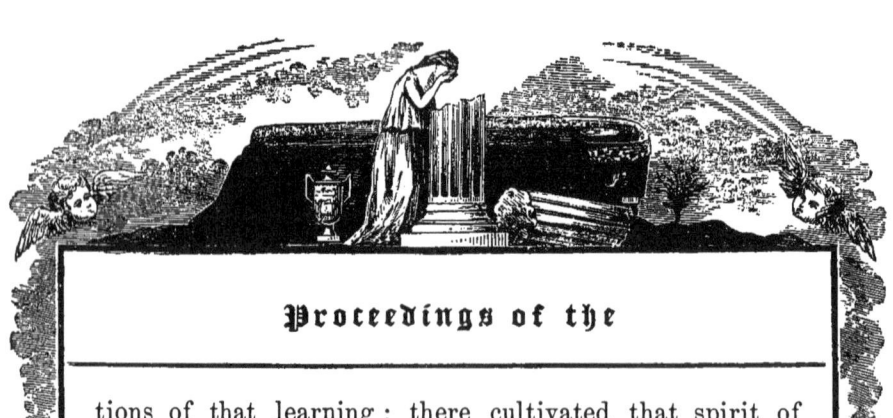

Proceedings of the

tions of that learning; there cultivated that spirit of patient and thorough research, that diligent and exhaustive analysis, which became the sure guarantees of his future fame. The library was a large one for the country, complete, or nearly so, in English and American Reports, and from these numerous volumes Mr. HILL, with pains-taking diligence, selected the cases which bore upon his subjects and by careful discrimination and thoughtful study compelled, from conflicting decisions and distracted *dicta*, the subtle principle that governed them.

Much has been said, sometimes disparagingly, of the manner in which this work is constructed. Two large volumes of discursive notes, appended to one volume of text, seem indeed disproportionate, and the work would undoubtedly have given more general satisfaction had it been a fresh treatise. But portions of the notes had been already printed when Mr. HILL began his labors, and the materials increased upon the hands of both the editors to an extent far beyond their original conceptions. But no lawyer, it seems to me, can use this book long without being conscious of its great practical value, and coming to prize the clearness of its discussions, and the fidelity with which the numerous cases cited are digested. There are some heads of the law which are nowhere else so fully or so ably treated, as, for example, the head of the conclusiveness of judgments and decrees, as affected by the jurisdic-

New York Bar.

tion of the tribunals rendering them, the subject-matter involved, the parties named in the suit, and other kindred topics contained in the second volume of the notes, the volume in the preparation of which Mr. HILL had by far the largest share.

This work on Evidence was not published till 1839. The completion of it was interrupted by Mr. HILL's professional avocations, as he had some years previously opened an office in Saratoga Springs. This village was at that time quite a centre of judicial and professional activity. While Judge COWEN, at one end of it, was pursuing his laborious career, Chancellor WALWORTH, at the other, was toiling under the administration of the equity jurisdiction of the State. Judge WILLARD, then Circuit Judge and Vice Chancellor, also resided in the village. Many present doubtless, recollect with pleasure the summer terms held before the Chancellor, in his quiet office at the north end of the village. These terms naturally brought much equity business from abroad, and it was not long before Mr. HILL's services were in requisition. In the summer of 1839, in the case to which Mr. GERARD has alluded, of The People on the relation of Barry *vs.* Mercein, (reported in 8 Paige,) Mr. HILL was employed by the relator, Mr. BARRY. The proceeding was instituted by Mr. BARRY to regain the custody of his infant child, withheld by its mother, who had left her husband, and was living with her

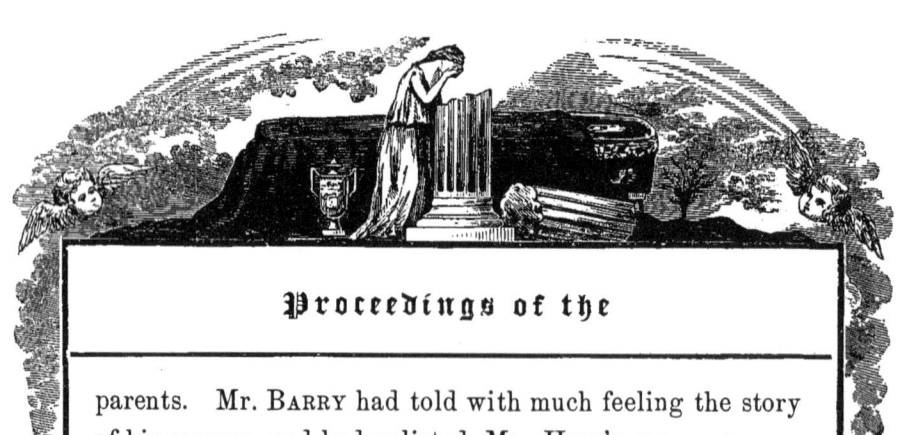

Proceedings of the

parents. Mr. BARRY had told with much feeling the story of his wrongs, and had enlisted Mr. HILL's warm sympathy. The reputation of the opposing counsel had preceded them. Mr. HILL had never before, I believe, encountered any of the leading lawyers of this city. He now threw all his energies into his preparation for the argument of this case, and well do I remember the pride which his younger associates felt in seeing him matched against the most eminent counsel at the bar, and witnessing the ability which he then displayed.

The discussions in this case, and the controversy growing out of Judge COWEN's refusal to discharge MCLEOD on *habeas corpus*, led to the valuable treatise on this writ, published by Mr. HILL in the appendix to the third volume of his Reports.

In 1840, Mr. HILL was appointed State Reporter; and after the preparation at Saratoga of one or two volumes of Reports, removed to Albany, with Judge COWEN's son, SIDNEY J. COWEN. The early death, a few years later, of this gentleman, at the opening of a brilliant career, left a place in Mr. HILL's firm which I was called to take. Again I became a witness to the same laborious honesty in the preparation of his Reports which I had seen bestowed on his earlier work. In selecting the cases to be reported, he regarded chiefly the permanent value of the decision, rejecting, so far as he felt himself at liberty to do so, every-

New York Bar.

thing of only local and fugitive interest. In preparing the cases for the press, he labored to compress the statements of facts into the smallest space, and removed from the opinions of the Judges such details as his own narrative rendered superfluous. He spent hours in condensing and remodeling the syllabus or head-note, till it should succinctly, clearly and accurately express the very point of the decision, and frequently added valuable discussions on kindred topics suggested by the reported case.

His reports have been very generally considered as models in every respect. No copyright price per volume could tempt him to swell their number, to heap into them masses of mere print, or to do his work hurriedly or negligently. They will bear the most rigid scrutiny as specimens of honest, faithful book-making.

Judge COWEN died early in 1844. His library had been brought to Albany by his son; and after the death of the latter, the settlement of his estate rendered the sale of it necessary. It was bought by Mr. CAGGER, who had just then dissolved a long connection with the late SAMUEL STEVENS. This library was one of many inducements that led to Mr. HILL's partnership with Mr. CAGGER. By this arrangement Mr. HILL avoided the loss of the books which had been so long his companions. The library has been kept in his office ever since, and thus for over twenty-five years it has been Mr. HILL's constant home. He had be-

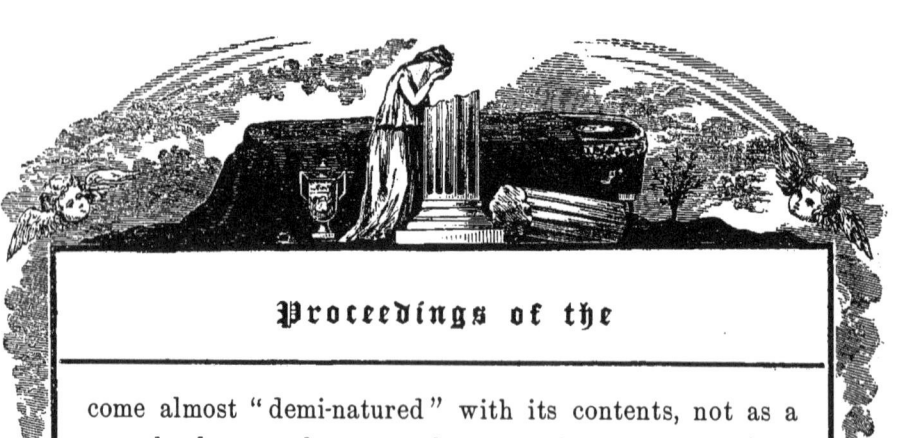

Proceedings of the

come almost "demi-natured" with its contents, not as a mere book-worm, however; he was rather an oracle of the law, of which these books supplied the flame.

Mr. HILL's professional business now rapidly increased, though the reputation of the late SAMUEL STEVENS and of Mr. MARCUS T. REYNOLDS, of Albany, was still at its height; and in 1845 he resigned his office of State Reporter. From this time he took rank among the acknowledged leaders of the bar, and his great merits as a lawyer became widely known. It is not necessary, therefore, that I should trace farther a career which has been justly characterized in "words fitly spoken" by gentlemen with whom it brought him in more direct contact. In looking back upon this career, however, I am reminded of MILTON's lines:

> "Fame is the spur the clear spirit doth raise,
>   (That last infirmity of noble mind)
> To scorn delights, and live laborious days;
>   But the fair guerdon when we hope to find,
> * * * * * * * * *
> Comes the blind Fury, with the abhorred shears,
>   And slits the thin-spun life."

Before his thin-spun life was cut short—a life that always seemed to have but a slender hold upon his spare and attenuated frame, Mr. HILL had found this "fair guerdon" of fame, so much of it at least as waits upon great lawyers; but I never thought that fame—such fame, at least, as in "broad rumor lies"—was the spur of his

New York Bar.

effort. Rather, I think, he was drawn on and enticed by an innate desire of perfection, of doing well and thoroughly whatever he undertook. He used none of the arts by which notoriety was accomplished. He forgot himself in his work.

If I spoke of Mr. HILL's qualities of intellect, I should probably betray some of that ardent admiration by which, when a youth, I was carried away; but the fond appreciation with which, as a student in his office, I looked up to what seemed to me his great intellectual ability, and the eminence which I then anticipated for him, are verified to-day.

I have heard it surmised that Mr. HILL was a mere lawyer. If by this is meant that his intellectual activity was chiefly in the walks of his profession, it is true; but it is not true that he had no tastes outside of that profession. He was familiar with the best English literature, and a lover of good books; and when he could throw off the thoughts of his work, he was a most delightful and genial companion. His tastes were refined, his sensibilities lively and delicate, his nature frank, and without guile, his heart warm and true. For myself, I can never forget how much I am indebted to him for example, guidance, encouragement, nor the unfailing kindness which, in boyhood, and ever afterwards, I always received from him.

Doubtless he gave himself up too exclusively to that

Proceedings of the New York Bar.

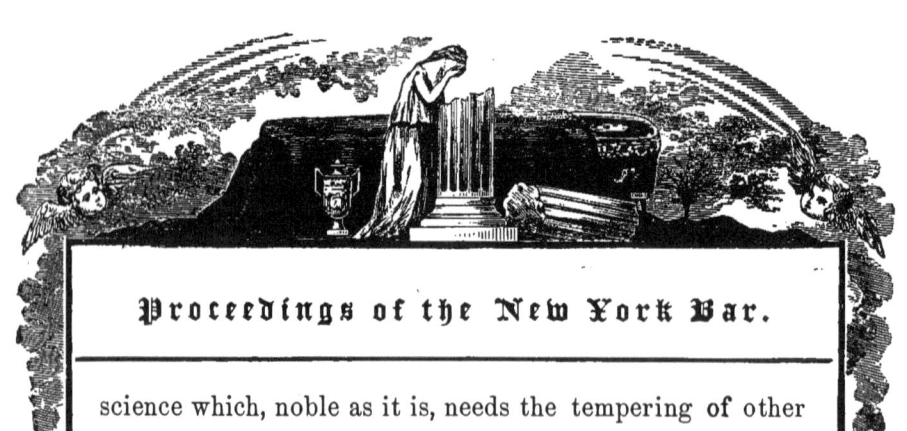

science which, noble as it is, needs the tempering of other studies; but Providence, in guiding each one of us to our vocation, seems to indicate that in it should our chief usefulness be looked for; and the devotee of the law is dedicated to a large obedience. To the high praise of Mr. HILL it may be truly said, that he practised his profession nobly, being above all low or sordid motives, all envy or detraction, and that he won the high position he attained, solely by the thorough, honest, faithful use of the fine faculties with which he was gifted.

Whereupon the question being put by the chair on the resolutions, they were unanimously adopted.

The chair appointed Mr. JOHN W. EDMONDS, Mr. GILBERT DEAN, and Mr. STEPHEN P. NASH, as the committee to communicate the proceedings of the meeting to the Court of Appeals.

And the meeting then adjourned.

Proceedings of the Albany Bar.

A VERY large meeting of the bar convened in the Court of Appeals room at 12 o'clock, noon.

Hon. LYMAN TREMAINE, Attorney-General, moved that Judge JOHNSON, Chief Judge of the Court of Appeals, preside, which was agreed to.

J. V. L. PRUYN, Esq., and CLARK B. COCHRANE, Esq., were appointed Secretaries.

ATTORNEY GENERAL TREMAINE

then addressed the meeting as follows :

MR. CHAIRMAN AND BRETHREN : An acknowledged leader of our profession has fallen! He, whose varied and extensive legal attainments were universally acknowledged— he, who in his professional contests was never defeated when he was entitled to succeed by the merits of his cause —he, who was the victor in so many hard-fought intellectual combats—he, whose superior in all the element that constitute the eminent lawyer and the accomplished jurist, can not, in my humble judgment, be found at the American bar—has finally been arrested in his career; and in the struggle with an adversary more powerful than any he had before encountered, has been vanquished and slain upon the field of battle! No enemy in human form has accomplished this work! It required a superhuman foe—the conqueror of princes and of emperors—of statesmen and of orators—of warriors and of heroes—one more powerful than Cicero or Demosthenes, than Cæsar, or Alexander, or Bonaparte!

We, who are the mourning survivors in the profession which had the distinguished honor of claiming NICHOLAS HILL as one of its members, have assembled on this occasion to take some suitable notice of our bereavement.

We have not met to pronounce that elaborate eulogium upon the deceased which is so eminently due to his life and character. To us, who knew him so intimately, that would seem wholly unnecessary, either to perpetuate his greatness or to preserve the memory of his virtues. We remember his modest and untiring nature, and it seems to us that, if his own wishes during life could have been consulted, they would have pointed to a less ostentatious method of exhibiting our affection and regard.

With such views we meet to-day. We would condole with each other upon our great loss—we would derive some consolation in this hour of affliction from the con-

Albany Bar.

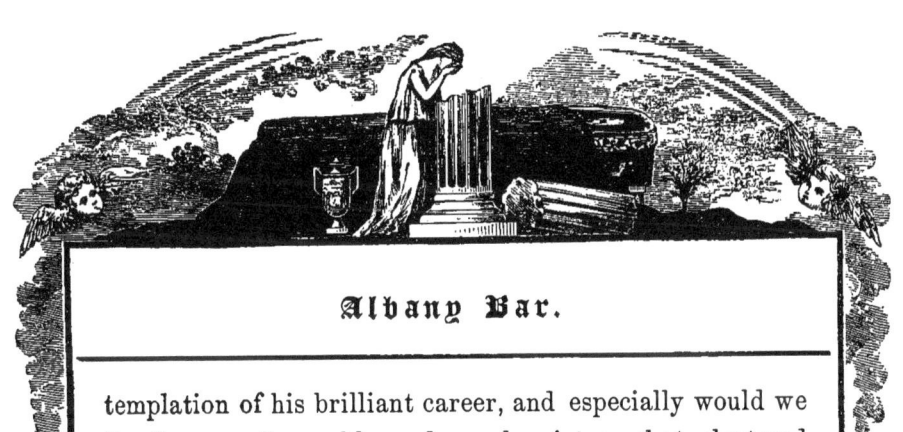

templation of his brilliant career, and especially would we dwell upon the noble and manly virtues that clustered around his brow.

We come as friends, as brothers, as members of the same professional family. We come to mingle our sympathies together—to sweeten the bitter contents of the cup that is presented to our lips—to weave a few garlands of flowers with the cypress branches to be laid upon his grave.

The occasion seems appropriate to make a brief allusion to those traits of character which had placed Mr. HILL in the high and commanding position at the bar, that he ocenpied at the time of his death. When I first knew Mr. HILL, he was in the full tide of an extensive and successful practice, and had laid the foundations of that enviable reputation which he finally attained. Both of us passed a portion of our clerkship in the office, and under the instructions of the same lawyer. I remember well with what earnestness and enthusiasm this gentleman was wont to speak of the ability and tact that had been exhibited by Mr. HILL during his clerkship in his office. He took great pride in his professional success, and often alluded to it as affording a complete fulfillment of his early predictions in reference to one whom he pleasantly called his "boy."

From such a commencement, Mr. HILL advanced, step by step, with sure and steady progress, by severe discipline and persevering study, up through the different stages of his profession, until at last he reached the highest round in the ladder of professional eminence. I think I do no injustice to the eminent and illustrious lawyers who were Mr. HILL's cotemporaries, in declaring the opinion that when death marked him for his victim, he was retained to argue more causes in the Court of Appeals than any lawyer in the State, and that among his professional acquaintances, and on the bench, he exercised an influence and commanded a respect scarcely equaled, and certainly not surpassed.

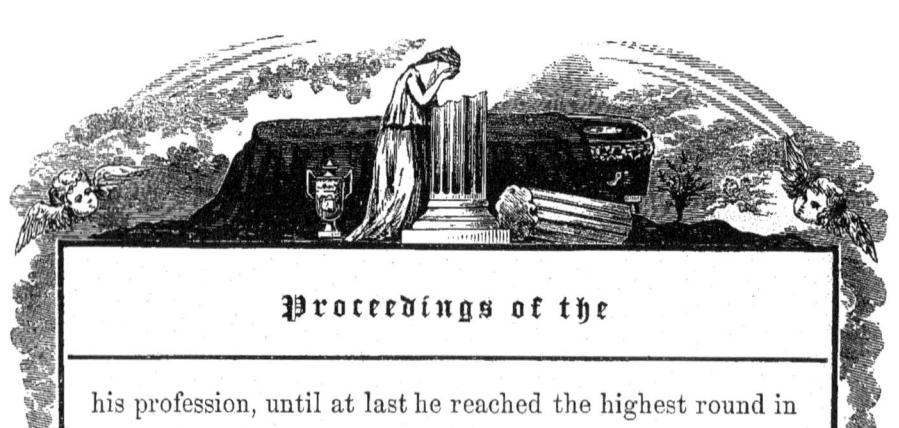

If the youthful aspirants for professional honors should ask me by what means he reached this position and acquired this influence, I should answer, that it was only by severe study, by continuous untiring labor, and by the unremitting application of all the energies of a strong and vigorous intellect to the profession which he loved.

He possessed a mind imbued with strong common sense. He was, in moments of relaxation, overflowing with wit, humor and pathos. In his forensic arguments, however, he rarely availed himself of the aid which these qualities furnished. In early life, he was deemed a most formidable antagonist before a jury at *Nisi Prius*. Of late years, however, he had abandoned the field to his younger partner, and confined his labors to arguments before the Court. Here he found congenial employment. Here he was always at home.

Albany Bar.

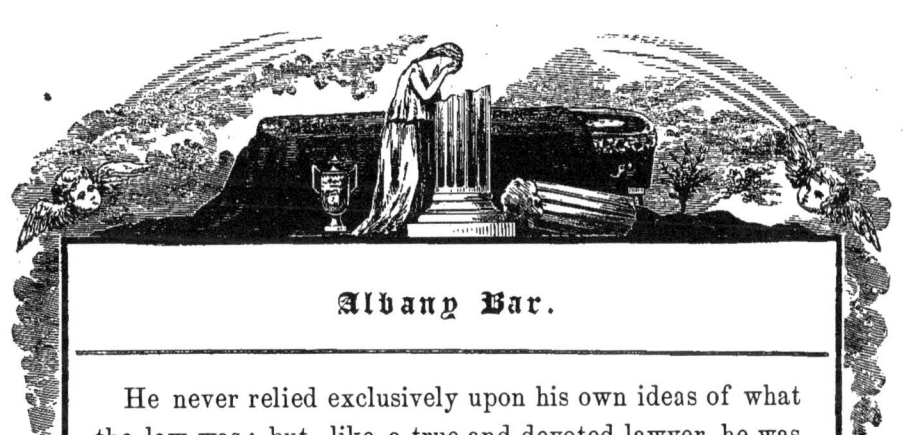

He never relied exclusively upon his own ideas of what the law was; but, like a true and devoted lawyer, he was willing to subject his own impressions to the test of adjudication. He did not profess to be wiser than the great luminaries whose wisdom and learning have been contributing, for centuries, to establish and improve the body of the Common Law. He did not believe that all wisdom was monopolized by the present age and generation, nor did he think he could reach conclusions with unerring accuracy by intuition or his own unaided reason. He was, therefore, in its fullest sense, a student. Possessing one of the finest law libraries in this country, he never wearied with digging among its hidden treasures for that knowledge which was necessary to satisfy himself, and particularly to enable him to satisfy the Court. No miner was ever more persevering and enthusiastic in searching for gold than was he in his pursuit of learning. No lover was ever more devoted to his mistress than was Mr. HILL to his profession. Such industry produced its fruits.

He was a walking library. Never satisfied with his search until he had traced a principle to its source, and ascertained the reason upon which it was founded, and then pursued it in all its ramifications and modifications, his mind became a well filled storehouse of legal knowledge. You could not apply to him for information upon any branch of legal science connected with the Common, Civil

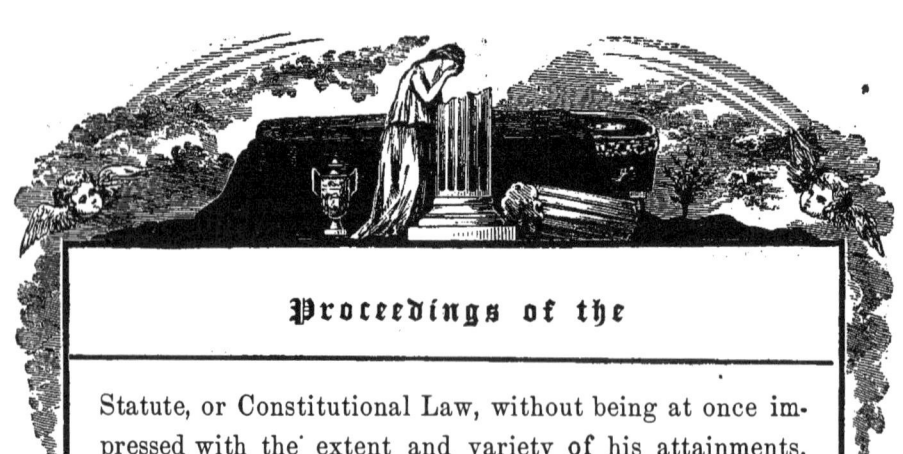

Statute, or Constitutional Law, without being at once impressed with the extent and variety of his attainments. Indeed, my conviction of truth requires that I should add, that if he erred at all, it was in the depth and extent of his devotion to his profession. It was in allowing this to become too absorbing, and thereby encroaching upon the time which could have been conferred upon society with so much advantage to it, and possibly too, disregarding the laws of recreation and of health. He resolved, however, to stand at the head of his profession, and long since he had accomplished his purpose.

But while we do homage to his accomplishments as a learned lawyer, what shall I say of him as a citizen—as a companion—as a man? No person can do justice to this branch of my theme, unless he has had the high privilege of associating with him in those occasional periods when all care was thrown aside. Then the real goodness of his nature was seen and appreciated. On such occasions he resigned himself to the spirit of the hour with an abandon that was charming. He became playful as a child. His genial characteristics won your regard, while his cheerful mirthfulness became irresistibly contagious. You saw before you not the grave lawyer whose ability and learning swayed the decrees of Courts, but only the merry and lively comrade whose gravity, if it was put on, was only

Albany Bar.

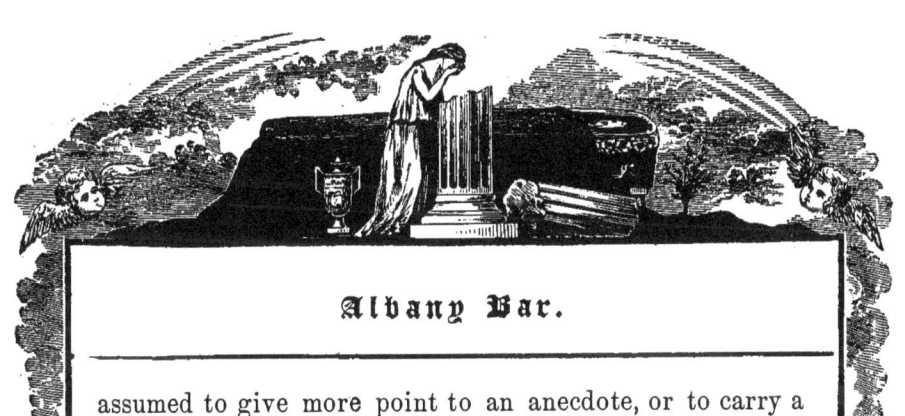

assumed to give more point to an anecdote, or to carry a jest home to its destination.

Death is rarely a welcome visitor.. In this instance, however, it is doubtful whether it could have come at a period more unobjectionable, so far as relates to the reputation of its illustrious victim. The loss will be mainly that of his family, for whom he would have preferred that his life could have been prolonged, and of the public, who will scarcely be able to supply his place. He died in the full zenith of his professional fame. He had reached its summit. He died before the corroding finger of advancing age had touched his mental faculties, or dimmed the clearness of his intellectual vision. He died, as I think he would have preferred to die, in the field of his active labors, and with the harness on. No long and wasting disease preceded his dissolution; but while he was full of hope for recovery from illness, his spirit passed to the other world quietly, peacefully, and like one calmly going to sleep.

Let us cherish the memory of his virtues. Let us strive to imitate those rare qualities which enabled him to die without an enemy. Let us cultivate that ingenuous frankness which was one of the secrets of his influence and power. I take this occasion to suggest to my brethren of this city the propriety of obtaining a full length portrait of Mr. HILL, to adorn the walls of this room, between the portraits of ABRAHAM VAN VECHTEN and DANIEL CADY.

Proceedings of the

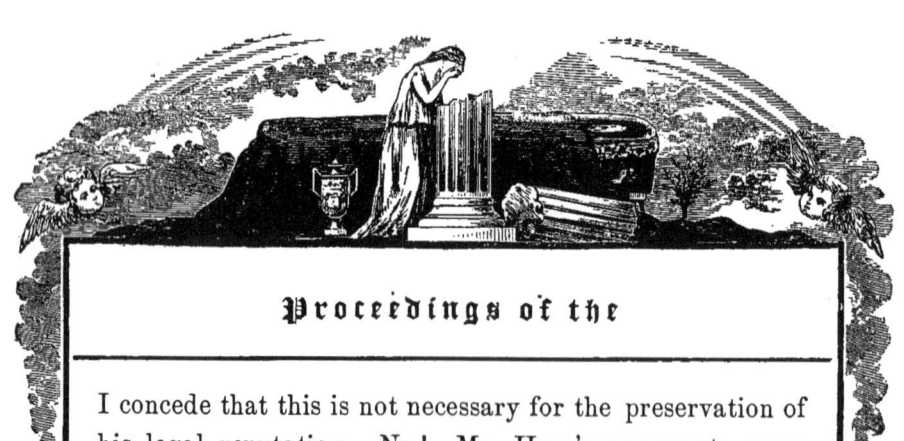

I concede that this is not necessary for the preservation of his legal reputation. No! Mr. HILL's arguments, or so much of them as has been preserved, his connection with the leading cases for many years, the monuments of his industry and learning as an author and reporter, have identified his name with the legal history of this State, and there it will forever remain. But our really great lawyers are becoming so like angel visits, that it seems to me that we should have Mr. HILL's likeness before us, in the Court room, to stimulate the rising generation of lawyers to follow his example. If the suggestion meets with your approval, it will afford me great pleasure to unite with you in accomplishing that object.

We are forcibly reminded by this sad event of the tendency to sudden death created by the confinement and absorbing nature of our professional pursuits. Is it not the part of wisdom to pay more heed to the laws of health, to play more and work less? But especially, is it not our duty to conduct ourselves in such a way that death will never find us unprepared? We believe that "the trumpet shall sound and the dead shall be raised incorruptible, and we shall be changed. For this corruption must put on incorruption, and this mortal must put on immortality."

> "Determined are the days that fly
> Successive o'er thy head,
> The numbered hour is on the wing
> That lays thee with the dead.

Albany Bar.

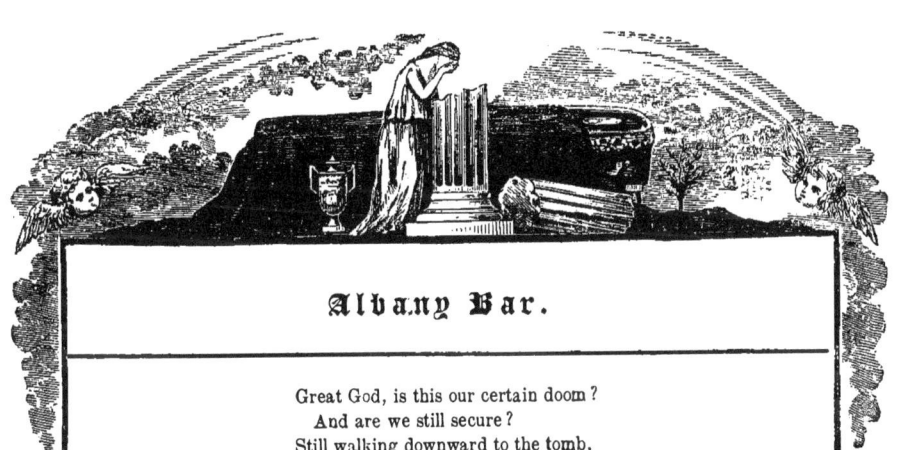

> Great God, is this our certain doom?
> And are we still secure?
> Still walking downward to the tomb,
> And yet prepare no more?"

In conclusion, I move that a committee of seven be appointed by the Chairman to report resolutions expressive of the sense of this meeting.

Proceedings of the Troy Bar.

A MEETING of the members of the bar of Rensselaer County was held at the Court House, in the city of Troy, on the 6th instant, to express their regret at the death of the late distinguished NICHOLAS HILL.

W. A. BEACH, Esq.,

then addressed the meeting as follows:

The occasion which collects us is no ordinary one. Our presence here is no unfeeling formality. Our offering to-day is not mere lip service—the vacant ceremonial of custom. The calamities of life often arrest attention for a moment, in our hurried and tumultuous progress. We pause awhile, and look upward and beyond the transitory things of earth, startled into deep but transient consciousness of the immortal within us. The cares and aspirations and duties of the world soon erase the impression. Careless of the monition, we quickly resume our place in the long procession of earth-worshipers, and with heart as light, and step as eager as ever, chase the gilded phantoms of time. Not such will be the influence of the death of

Proceedings of the Troy Bar.

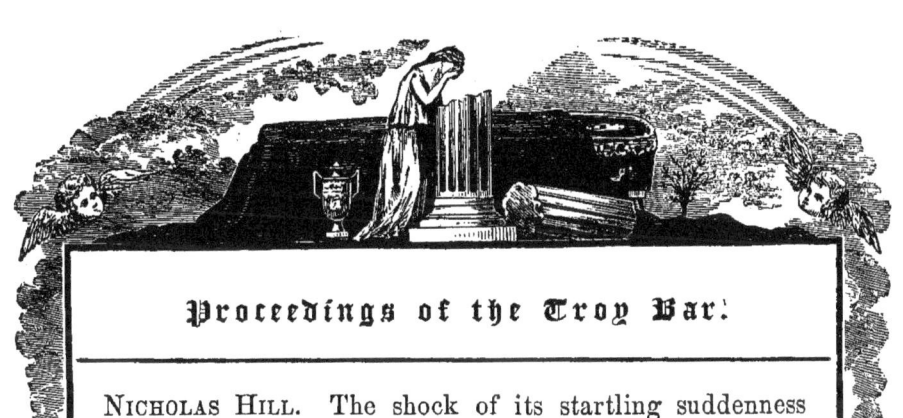

NICHOLAS HILL. The shock of its startling suddenness may pass away, but its moral will remain forever. In his death we see, too, his life. The passionate sorrow of this hour will subside, but his memory, with genial and ennobling influence, will abide with us while virtue shall be respected and worth honored. We shall remember him as he moved among us in all the grandeur of his intellectual nature, and remembrance will be keener as we think that his step is silent forever. In his life there was influence, but his death gives to the lessons of his noble career, high emphasis and power. For many years we have seen his enthusiastic professional devotion, and its efforts and its triumphs. We have drawn inspiration from his example, and felt the stir of exciting emulation as we watched his brilliant achievements. But how more vividly, to-day, the lustre of his great life beams upon us. Its teachings speak to us with weightier significance. We see more clearly his striking characteristics. We feel more deeply their value. So true it is that Death gilds and intensifies the character of real greatness.

In this presence, it is superfluous to speak of the professional character of Mr. HILL. With it all of us are familiar. It needs no demonstration of eulogy. With common accord we recognize it as the true standard of excellence. Why speak of his varied acquirements, embellishing the sterility of severe legal argument—of his exhaustless and exhausting research—of the resource and felicity of his illustration—of his terse, epigrammatic diction—of his enthusiasm, which rested not till it stood by the limpid fountains of principle, and could read truth unerringly? All these, are they not written on the hearts of his brethren?

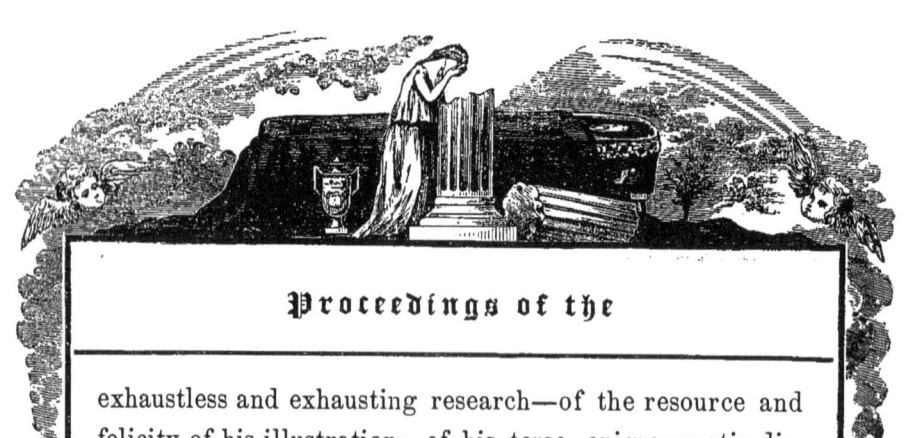

Others may admire his genius and attainments; may remember him as a gifted and glorious intellect, ennobling and adorning both our profession and our common nature.

I prefer to think of him with fonder and more familiar associations.

Long years ago, in the sunny day of early manhood, I knew him.

Ere his name was carved by his own hand among the highest aspirants along the rocky steep of professional renown, we sported together at the base of the constellated mount. From thence onward through the wasting years, we have been linked in warmest friendship. Great as he was in legal acquirements—symmetrical and graceful as was his professional character—I loved and admired him most as the companion and friend. After all, his greatness was rather of his heart than his head. From his soul came the instincts, animating and directing his mental exertion, making him in all that was generous, truthful and noble, the BAYARD of our profession. No one truly understood him who had not mingled sympathies in hours of social re-

Troy Bar.

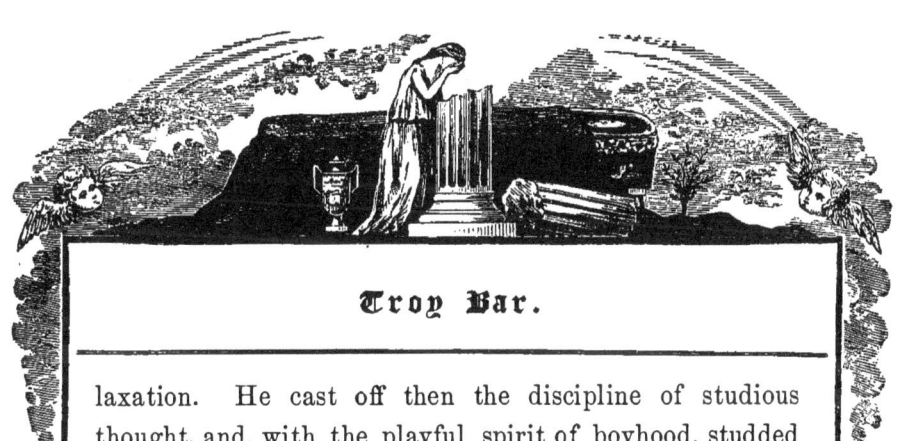

laxation. He cast off then the discipline of studious thought, and, with the playful spirit of boyhood, studded the brilliant hours with the rarest gems of fancy and wit. Not alone in the learning of his profession was his mind enriched. Literature and poetry embellished it. Historic lore dignified it : it was filled with the incidents and anecdotes of biography : it had mastered the great truths of governmental and political science. Scarce any department of knowledge from which his unwearied industry had not gathered gems and flowers. From these copious stores he garlanded the scenes of social and friendly intercourse. With lively imagination, a keen apprehension and ready retort, his pleasant hours were full of mental activity. He loved the conflict of mind. The giant stooped to play with the lighter armor of intellect, but his heart gave tone to his merry satire. He was simple, guileless and cheerful. Too lofty to be envious, and too kind to be harsh, his racy humor and sportive sarcasm left no sting behind.

Such was he in his companionship. How trusty and generous he was in friendship, many there be who can bear him testimony. Whoever won his respect and love, commanded his countenance and effort. His was not the friendship of calculation or convenience : it sought congenial spirit. Disdaining meanness himself, his associations were with the noble and true of heart. His pure, upright nature instinctively discovered the good, and wel-

Proceedings of the Troy Bar.

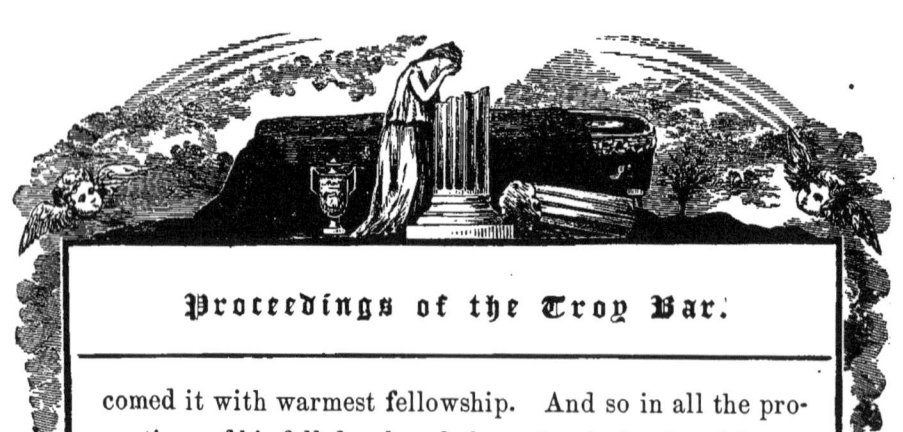

comed it with warmest fellowship. And so in all the proportions of his full developed character, in head and heart, his instincts and sympathies, his learning and its fruit, were all goodness and truth.

Fitting is it, therefore, that we who honored and loved him should stand in reverent grief beside his bier. Becoming is it that the hush of awe and sorrow should overspread the busy activities of life. No wonder that his death should awaken a common emotion of profoundest sadness and grief. The lofty and lowly, the gifted and humble among us, have each and all a friend, a companion an exemplar—to mourn. No more will his dim-closed eyes flash upon us the radiance of his glorious immortality. No more will his cold, pale lip enchant us with the melody of thought. The kindly grasp of his honest hand will welcome us no more on earth. We call him dead; and yet he is not. With him death is but another life. Nay, it is but manifold life; life immortal beyond the grave; and life with each of us, so long as loving hearts can cherish the memory of the good and great.

> "Can that man be dead
> Whose spiritual influence is on his kind?
> He lives in glory; and his speaking dust
> Has more of life than half its breathing moulds."

Proceedings of the Court of Appeals.

ALBANY, JUNE 7, 1859.

THE Court of Appeals met at the Capitol at ten o'clock yesterday. Present: Judges JOHNSON, COMSTOCK, SELDEN, DENIO, STRONG, ALLEN, GRAY and GROVER. There was a very full attendance of the bar. A number of prominent citizens, including Governor MORGAN, Comptroller CHURCH, and others, were also present.

Immediately on the opening of the Court,

MR. JOHN H. REYNOLDS

rose, and formally announced to their Honors the death of the lamented NICHOLAS HILL, coupling it with a tribute to the character of the deceased, both professional and personal, so eloquent as to touch the hearts of all the auditory with the deep emotions which the speaker himself evinced. He spoke as follows:

MAY IT PLEASE YOUR HONORS: Since the last meeting of this Court, one who has been accustomed to welcome your return has suddenly been called away. His place at this bar is vacant, and will be filled by him no more forever.

Proceedings of the

While yet busy in the great labors of his life, and in the very fullness of his intellectual stature, Nicholas Hill has unexpectedly left the employments of earth, and entered upon the realities of another life. His departure from among us was so sudden, that those who were most intimately associated with his daily avocations were scarcely made aware of his illness before the sad intelligence of his death was announced. An event so mournful could not ail to arrest public attention, and spread deep sorrow over the hearts of all who knew and honored him. To none beyond his immediate family circle did this great bereavement seem more near than to his brethren at the Capitol, who were the constant associates of his professional life, and who were bound to him by the nearer relations of friendship and affection. To give expression to their feelings of respect and regard for his character, and sorrow for his death, they assembled together with mournful feelings, and adopted resolutions expressing in some slight degree their esteem for his worth, their admiration for his great character as a lawyer, and their regret for his sudden and untimely death. They gathered in reverent grief around his bier, and followed to its last resting place, in silence and tears, all that remained on earth of one so loved and honored. They desire to preserve some memorial of their regard for what he was, and I now present the record of their proceedings, with a request that, in respect to his

Court of Appeals.

memory, they be entered upon the minutes of this Court. It was in this place that he spent the later years of his life, and it is upon your records that the most enduring monuments of his labors exist; and we feel it to be appropriate that, upon the field of his professional fame, there shall remain a fitting testimonial to his great character. The last effort of his professional life was made in this presence. It terminated the labors of the last term of this honorable Court, and with him it was the close of a career that will be looked to as an example of all that can be achieved by a lofty intellect and unremitting labor. It was also the termination of a life crowded with all that is estimable in human character. I was with him as an adversary in his last public labor, in the profession that he loved and honored and adorned. I was with him as a friend in almost the last hours that he spent in this life, and I come here to-day to bring the tribute of his brethren to his exalted worth, and to add my own feeble expression of admiration for him as a lawyer, my reverence for his character as a man, and my affection for a lost associate and friend.

It is not necessary, in the presence of this court, to dwell upon the great qualities that formed the character of our lamented brother. You well know the measure of his luminous intellect and the noble qualities of his great nature. You have been delighted and instructed with his eloquence and learning. Every volume that records your

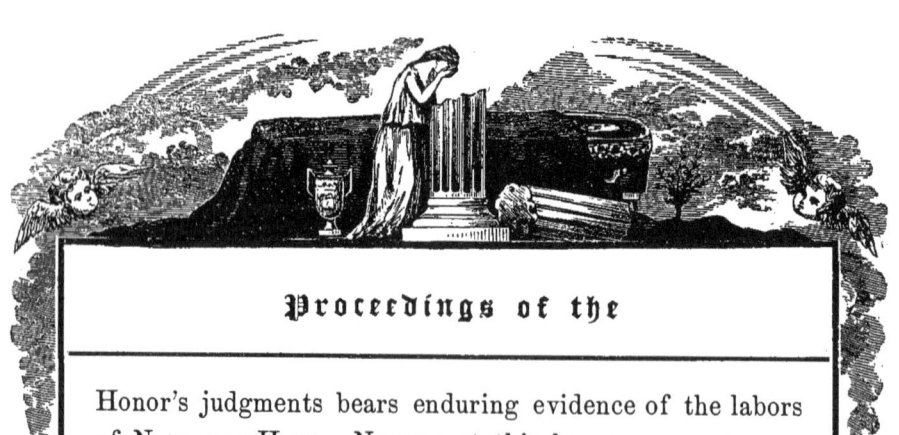

Honor's judgments bears enduring evidence of the labors of NICHOLAS HILL. No man at this bar ever spent more time in valuable discussion, and none ever brought to the consideration of any question a greater amount of exact legal learning, or presented in a more attractive and impressive form the severer logic of the law. He never undertook the discussion of any question that he had not fully investigated, and of which he had not, by attentive study and reflection, made himself the master. The leading thought of his life was his profession. He loved its labors with enthusiastic devotion. No temptation could seduce him from its pursuit. If he relaxed his severer studies, it was to beguile an hour in the freedom of social enjoyment, or amid the delights of literature. His was a life of intellectual toil and of intellectual triumph. He was indebted to no adventitious aid for the honors that he won. They were the results of his own unaided intellect and of his unparalleled industry. The reverence that we all feel for his great character, is but the just tribute we pay to exalted merit.

His whole life was devoted to the loftiest of human pursuits.

The administration of justice presents the noblest field for the exercise of human capacity. It forms, as has been said, the ligament which binds society together. Upon its broad foundation is erected the edifice of public liberty.

Court of Appeals.

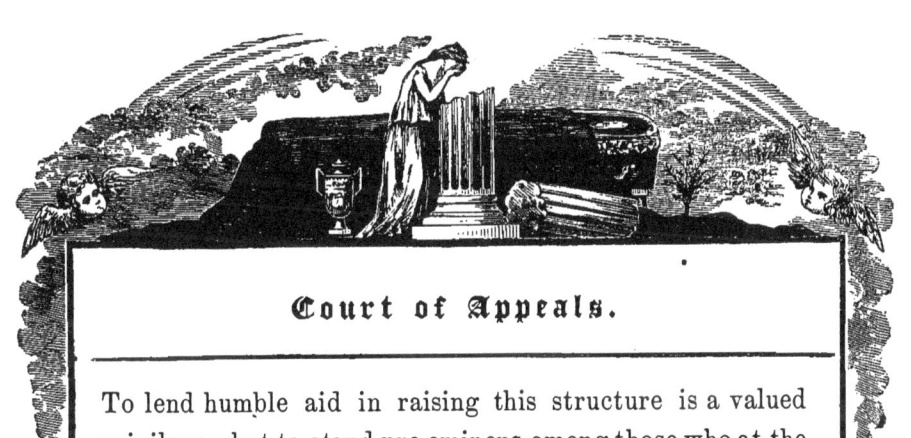

To lend humble aid in raising this structure is a valued privilege; but to stand pre-eminent among those who at the bar, or upon the bench, have beautified and adorned the Temple of Justice, is among the loftiest positions allotted to man. From that proud eminence, in the early morning of May, NICHOLAS HILL descended to the tomb—closing a spotless life in the full maturity of his power, in all the warmth of his affections, and while yet the sun of his existence seemed at noonday. To those who value truth and honor manhood, who reverence intellect, and love all that is generous and noble in human character, his memory will be cherished as among the most precious recollections of life, and by the purest and greatest of those who survive him, his example may be viewed with profit, and it will be well with any who, at the close of life, are worthy to fill a grave such as received all that was mortal of NICHOLAS HILL.

To most of all those with whom the name of our departed brother was familiar, he will be remembered only as a great lawyer. To some of us he will be cherished in a nearer and kindlier relation. Those he honored with his regard will prefer to think of him as he was when he withdrew from labor, and surrendered himself to the enjoyments of the hour. They will not forget his genial and generous nature, his graceful humor, the warmth of his friendship, and the thousand nameless qualities that made up the perfection of his character. Those who knew him only as the acknowledged leader of an honored profession, knew but little of the man. It was, when in the chosen circle of his friends, he left behind him his books and his briefs, that you were made acquainted with the excellent qualities of his heart. To those who knew him not, he may sometimes have seemed austere and distant; but to those he knew and loved, he was "sweet as summer." I prefer to cherish him as a valued friend, who has too early left us for an undiscovered country. I shall long remember our last interview on the last day of his life. Disease had laid its heavy hand upon him, but his great mind was clear, and the energy and warmth of his affections had suffered no abatement. He felt conscious that he had been overtasked, and, I think, regret, that he had subjected his frail organization to such unremitting and exhausting toil. But he looked forward to the return of health, and to a season of repose; and yet there was a lingering doubt in his own mind if that day would ever come. Alas! it never came. Within a few hours he passed from sleep to death, and there remains of him but the record of his toil and triumphs, and the memory of what he was. He died in the meridian of manhood, a victim to his own ceaseless devotion to the profession that now mourns his loss.

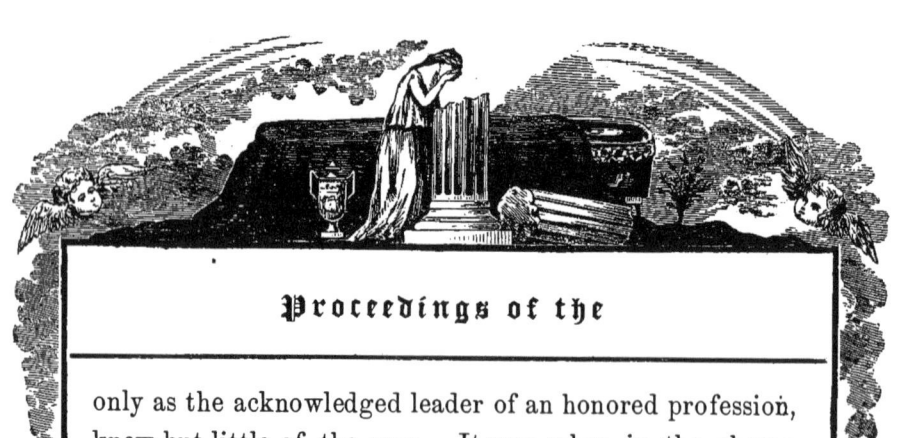

> "So the struck eagle, stretched upon the plain,
> No more through rolling clouds to soar again;
> Viewed his own feather in the fatal dart,
> That winged the shaft which quivered in his heart."

Court of Appeals.

However distinguished we may be, or have been, in this life, upon the bed of death, man returns to his individuality. He must die unaided and unsupported by human effort. Neither the applause of his fellow men nor the affection of friends and kindred, can support him in that hour. All the honors of earth are then as valueless to the possessor as the withered leaves which the winds of autumn will scatter over his grave. Those who sit in the judgment-seat and dispense human justice, will, in their turn, bow to that fixed and unalterable law of being which dedicates all that is mortal to decay and death. In view of that solemn hour, the impressive lesson of the life and death of him we mourn, will not pass unheeded. It comes too near us to be viewed with unconcern. I need not pause to impress it upon the attention of those who but yesterday looked into the new made grave of him who, according to the standard of human judgment, was entitled to "crown a life of labor with an age of ease;" but to whom, in the mysterious providence of God, it was not permitted to find rest from his labors, except amid the habitations of the dead.

In that silent resting place we leave him to the rewards which are promised to the pure in spirit, the blameless in life, and to the upright in heart.

At the conclusion of Mr. REYNOLDS' address, Judge EDMONDS presented the proceeding of the New York city bar, on the same subject, accompanying the duty assigned to him by appropriate remarks.

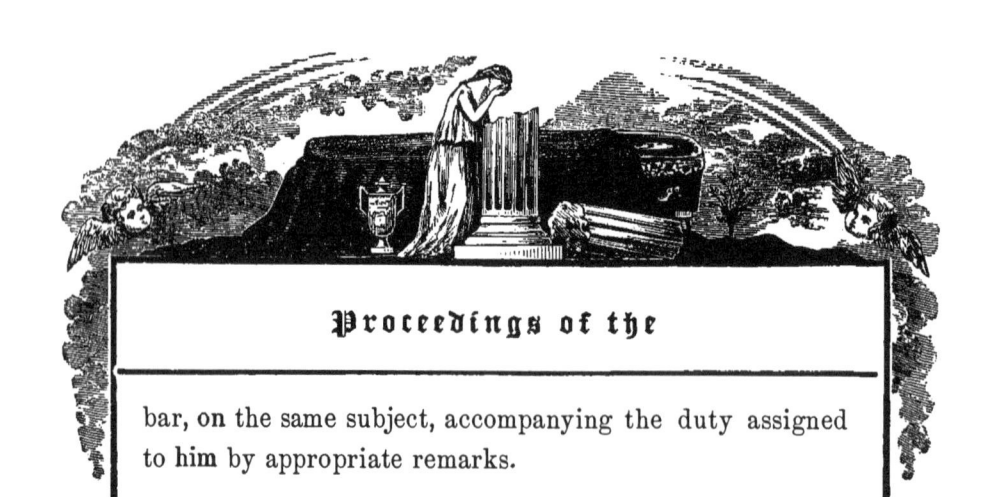

CHIEF JUDGE JOHNSON

responded on behalf of the Court, in the following words:

The warm and deserved tribute which has just been paid to the memory of our deceased friend and brother, receives an assenting response from the hearts of all those in whose hearing it has been pronounced, and will receive the same response from all who knew him. For more than twenty years NICHOLAS HILL has occupied an eminent position at the bar of this State. During the twelve years of the existence of this Court, he has at all times been largely concerned in its business, and of late has argued nearly one quarter of the causes orally debated. With the character of his mind, the Judges were thus made intimately acquainted, while his admirable, moral and social qualities warmed into affectionate regard the respect and admiration which his intellectual abilities commanded. It is not necessary, for the information of any who hear me, that I should speak of the care and labor which he bestowed upon the discharge of all his professional duties. He was never satisfied until he had exhausted all the resources of learning and reflection upon any subject which duty required him to examine. He made no parade of learning; so much

Court of Appeals.

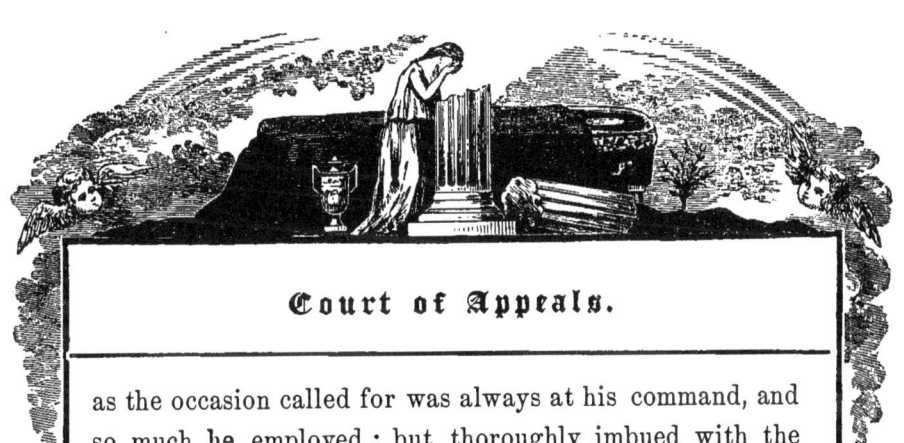

as the occasion called for was always at his command, and so much he employed; but thoroughly imbued with the principles of the law, it was his delight to rest his cases upon them. He had so great reverence for the law itself, and felt so deeply its harmonious structure, that he would rather have failed of success than have won it by trenching upon a sound rule. His arguments were therefore marked, no less by the masterly handling of legal principles, than by the entire candor and fairness with which he encountered the difficulties standing in his way.

In his intercourse with his fellow lawyers, he was full of courtesy and kindness, and was ever ready to sacrifice his own convenience to their accommodation. He was a man of entire integrity, of unflinching courage, of perfect truth, and, therefore, adorned all the relations of life, and enjoyed the esteem and regard which conduct so regulated is sure to win.

With the members of the bar his business relations were so extended, and his personal acquaintance so valued, that the death of no one among their number would have caused so much disarrangement of public business, or so deep and wide-spread grief.

It is right and becoming that the death of such a man should be marked by all the honors which it is in our power to pay to his memory, not alone for the consolation which is afforded to our own feelings, by the expres-

Proceedings of the Court of Appeals.

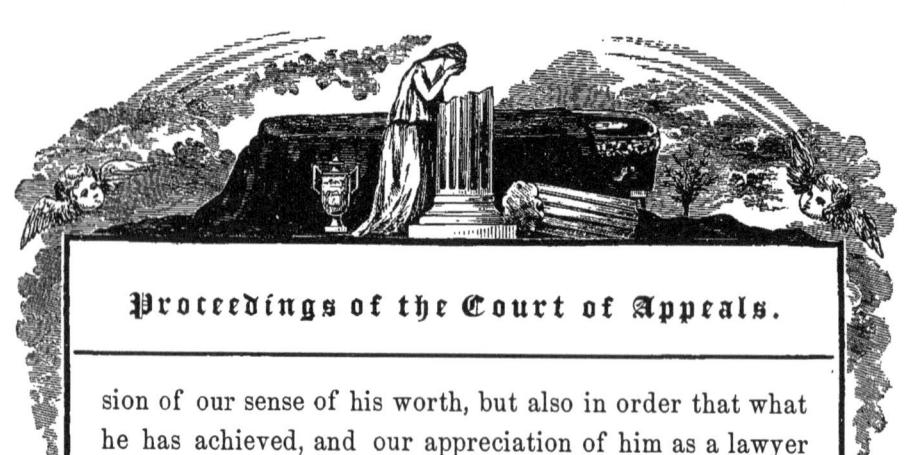

sion of our sense of his worth, but also in order that what he has achieved, and our appreciation of him as a lawyer and a man, may go down together to those who shall come after us, and may serve, so long as reverence for the law shall endure, to stimulate virtuous ambition by the teachings of his example.

We do, therefore, order, that the proceedings of the several meetings of the bar which have been this day presented, be entered of record on the minutes of this Court, with a relation of what has been said here on the part of the bar and the court.

The following order was then entered on the minutes:

IN THE COURT OF APPEALS, JUNE 7, 1859.—The death of the late NICHOLAS HILL having been formally announced to this Court by JOHN H. REYNOLDS, the Judges deem it proper to express their deep sympathy with the family of the lamented deceased, his associates at the bar, and the public, in which he lived and labored, for the great loss all have sustained in this sudden and unexpected bereavement.

They also express their high estimate of his great legal attainments and his exemplary deportment in all the social relations.

They direct that these expressions be entered on the records of this Court, and that a copy, signed by all the Judges, be sent to the family of the deceased.